How to Change
Your Karma
Now

Rita Panahi, L.Ac., Dipl.O.M.

ISBN: 978-0-9996648-8-9
First Edition: Oct 2019

10% of all author royalties are donated to the poor

Dedicated to:

Mata Amritanandamayi –

Embodiment of love and compassion

Nature – that gives us life

&

My Family

Rita Panahi, L.Ac., Dipl.O.M

To the Reader

T his book is for informational purposes only. The author and/or publisher are not accountable or responsible for the use or misuse of the information contained in this book and disclaim any liability to any party for any loss, damage, or disruption caused by errors or omissions, whether such errors or omissions result from negligence, accident, or any other cause.

The book is not intended as a substitute for medical advice and no claims are made that the information herein will alleviate health or any other serious life problems. The therapeutic procedures in this book are based on the personal experiences and studies of the author. The author is not responsible for any adverse effects resulting from use of any suggestions made in this book. If you have any medical conditions requiring attention, you should consult with your health care professional.

"You can't cross the sea
merely by standing and staring at the water."

— Rabindranath Tagore

Table of Contents

To the Reader v

Introduction ix

Chapter 1 What Is Karma? 1

Chapter 2 Clutter and Karma 21

Chapter 3 Your Body and Your Karma 39

Chapter 4 Making Amends to Change Karma 63

Chapter 5 Thoughts, Emotions, and Karma 85

Chapter 6 Heal Your Karma through Nature 105

Chapter 7 Giving—The Secret of Karma 121

Chapter 8 Plant Your Visions 139

Conclusion 153

Afterword 167

About the Author 175

Rita Panahi, L.Ac., Dipl.O.M

Introduction

S ometimes it might seem that no matter what you do, nothing changes in your life. Maybe you can't quit your unfulfilling or underpaid job because you haven't been able to find another opportunity. Maybe you have the same arguments with your spouse over and over, or maybe you haven't met your life partner yet and you're tired of dating. Maybe you've been struggling financially for years—but no matter how hard you work, you can't get your head above water to take a breath. Maybe you are tired of yourself, your repetitive emotional cycle that makes you continually frustrated or angry or sad or depressed. Maybe you desperately want to move to a new city but don't see how to make that possible. Maybe you are trying to lose weight or overcome a chronic health issue, but never seem to make sustainable progress.

Life can feel as if it is out of our hands at times—or it may feel like that all of the time. We may feel like a puppet in the hands of God or the universe, taking punches without having a say in how we want our lives to unfold.

Many aspects of my life were a constant struggle for years on end. Everything, each day, felt like an uphill battle. Willing to try any solution, I turned to many different resources—from spiritual and psychological guidance, to self-help courses, to traveling. I was looking for a way to change the direction my life was going. Sometimes I was reduced to tears of helplessness over the belief that certain things simply would not change despite my best efforts.

I felt at a loss for a long time before life finally took a turn for the better. Slowly but surely, I saw positive changes which pushed my life in the direction that I had always wished for. After climbing out of what felt like a deep hole, I realized that many people around me were struggling and suffering in the same ways that I had; in their careers, their relationships, their financial status, their health, and so on. Some even expressed envy of the new path I had created for myself and asked what I was doing to experience less struggle and more happiness. That's when I began to reflect back, to discern what exactly had initiated the change of direction in my life. I looked back on specific steps I had taken and what had worked to transform my karma from what seemed like a difficult and joyless existence to the more peaceful life I had dreamed of. Those steps are the focus of this book.

This is an interactive book, meaning that it requires you to take action. Simply reading it will benefit you somewhat, since awareness is the first step towards any change; however, it is through putting this information into practice that you will begin to see changes in your life. Change is a process that needs to happen on many levels. Simply wishing it will not get you from New York to Paris. Each step that you follow in this book will be a step closer to your destination. Even if you take just one step, that one step will benefit you in the long run. However, the more you apply these recommendations in your life, the more you will see results, as they will create a greater change in your karma—the same way that pulling out one weed will not prepare the soil of your garden for planting. Creating change requires numerous stages of preparation.

Some of the steps may be easy for you, while some will be a little more challenging. Do whatever works for you in the present moment and skip over the difficult parts. You can come back to those at a later time. The goal of this book is to help you to understand how karma works and feel empowered to overcome the obstacles in your life that make you feel stuck. Rather than blaming fate, I hope that you can find ways to create the life that you dream of by changing the direction of your karma.

I wish you abundance, happiness, positive energies, great health, peace, and for you to know that you are able to create such karma for yourself.

Chapter 1
What Is Karma?

"Every action of our lives touches on some chord that will vibrate in eternity."
— Edwin Hubbel Chapin

The word "karma" is often referred to as the law of cause and effect. What many don't realize, though, are the subtleties of karma, or the cause, and or how it's created. Karma is not only the result of our actions bearing fruit nor is it merely random forces, but more precisely it is the result of both conscious and unconscious actions, thoughts, emotions emotions—whether expressed or not expressed, —and the actions of those close to us, such as our parents, children, and spouse, and even of our ancestors. There are many levels to understanding karma.

When we experience a misfortune in our life, we either blame another person, or ourselves (without understanding the underlying cause within ourselves), or astrology, our parents, destiny, or fate. But blaming only disempowers us and does not point us in a direction to create change. When we begin to understand the depth of our responsibility and where we have failed to examine our part in the misfortune, we can take steps toward change and take our future, our karma, into our hands.

Take for example a certain karmic situation, such as a health condition. Some health conditions could have been avoided if we had taken better care of ourselves and made better lifestyle choices, while some health conditions are genetic and cannot be cured. Blaming our fate for the cold that we caught after hiking through the snow with shorts on doesn't make any sense. The same is true for karma. There are certain experiences we are fated to undergo, to learn and grow from; but many of the negative experiences we undergo are the consequence of prior improper choices we have made. So, if we were to make different choices, we could change our karma and our experiences.

To understand how to change karma, we first need to understand how we create it. We are a multi-layered existence with a physical body that expands into subtler forms of an energy body. Not only do our physical actions have an effect—such as our hand reaching out to touch someone, hit someone, or steal from someone—but also, in a similar way, our thoughts and emotions, whether expressed or not, send out vibrations into our surroundings. If those thoughts and emotions are about a specific person, it is certain that that person will feel those vibrations, whether or not they are sensitive enough to be aware of it. Thoughts and emotions are like an invisible telephone line sending messages to a targeted person or persons. Though we are individual beings, we are interconnected with all human beings, and even beyond, to all of nature and the universe. Just as your hand movement creates a wind within the air, so too thoughts and emotions send their vibrations as wind to their respective targets and throughout the universe.

This aspect of karma is what many people ignore, and as a result they are bewildered at negative experiences or when things simply don't go as they had hoped. Their external actions may not have shown any negativity, but their negative thoughts or emotions towards others manifested the negative cause that resulted in the negative effect. But since they were not aware of their thoughts or emotions, or even considered them as important factors, they blamed God, astrology, family, or fate for their circumstances. As a result, most karma is created out of ignorance, fear, and selfishness; ignorance, because many don't know what specifically creates karma, and fear and selfishness, because many see themselves as isolated entities and others as enemies, therefore inadvertently causing them harm.

When we experience love, there is more flow in our life. When we are in a state of fear, we feel trapped. Fear tends to contract and tighten. Love tends to allow and open.

Every action, thought, and emotion you have affects someone else's mind, emotions, and body in subtle and not so subtle ways and reflects back to us as energy that changes the direction of our karma. Let's say for example that you lie to someone about something significant. As is often the case, the truth reveals itself to that person, leaving them deeply hurt and angry. Even if they don't express it to you, they hold onto their angry thoughts. Anger is like a fire that has immense power. The anger that the person feels as a result of your lie will reach you, even if you are not aware of it. Then one day you get into a car accident. The car accident may seem to have nothing to do with your lie, but indirectly, your lie created a volcanic fire in another that is targeted at you energetically, unconsciously; and that created changes in your energy field which interfered with your peace of mind. Then you crashed your car, unsure of why you felt distracted while driving.

The things that happen to us, to a great extent, are a result of energy patterns we have created in the past. But because karma doesn't flow linearly, we cannot connect what is happening in the present to something that occurred a few years ago, or even a week ago. Maybe you got a divorce and, out of anger and greed, you lied in order to receive more money from your spouse. Then you succeeded and lived on happily, only to have someone come and rob your house a decade later or to contract an illness that does not allow you to enjoy the money you took. If something happens to us that we are unhappy with, we should always ask ourselves, *when did I do this to someone else?* It doesn't matter how far back on our life's timeline it took place.

Lastly, a dimension of karma that is even more rarely addressed is the karma of our ancestors and our parents, and how that ripples into our life. This holds true even if we were adopted. Any action, thought, or emotion leaves a mark. If our ancestors committed very grave wrongdoing, it may have remained in their energy field and got passed on to their children, and from their children to you. As such, you may find yourself a victim to the karma of your ancestors. In a similar way to how certain health conditions "run in the family," karma can be handed down as a result of energetic patterns and habits passed on from generation to generation, with no one having the awareness to undo the cause that created the effect.

So you see that the impact of your actions can reverberate out towards your family, your community, your country, all of nature, and the entire planet. Therefore it's important to always remember, whatever you do will not only impact you, but your parents, relatives, children, grandchildren, and beyond, either directly or indirectly. With this knowledge, make your choices consciously and wisely.

> *The choices you make today are the consequences you will need to deal with tomorrow. Choose wisely with the future in mind.*

As another example, let's say a person leaves work feeling very stressed and stops by a bar for a drink. He ends up drinking too much and trips over the curb as he heads to his car, hitting his head. For the next month he is not able to work. Since he is the sole supporter of his family, they no longer have a source of income for the entire month. His wife, the children, his boss and company, and of course he himself all suffer as a consequence of his accident. One might say that that's life, and accidents like this can happen to anyone; but that is an excuse for not taking responsibility. There are many ways to deal with stress, but over-drinking is not the best. In the moment, all he probably thought about was himself and his stress and how to overcome it. Choosing to drink, he did not imagine anything bad would happen, even though often drinking in and of itself increases the chances of unexpected occurrences. He didn't consider that if something did happen to him, it would impact not only him, but his entire family.

We may wish to think that we are our own islands and whatever we do is our problem and ours alone, but that is far from the truth. Even if we get a mere headache, it doesn't only impact us, but our boss (if we choose to take a day off work), our coworkers (if we do go to work but are unable to fulfill our responsibilities), and our family (if we need caretaking due to our pain). The distress we cause others, knowingly or unknowingly, due to our irresponsible actions, will reverberate back to us at some point.

No matter what we do, the law of karma hunts us down. It is simply the law of life. There is an invisible knowingness within the span of the universe and, indeed, within all of creation. Our ancestors' karma brings us to today, and we carry the torch for those around us now, and for those here tomorrow and beyond. Our awareness and conscious choices impact the karma we create in the future and we can in fact undo, to a great extent, karma that we have unknowingly created thus far.

Up until today, most people have believed that actions alone are the causes that create effects. But, as I mentioned, our thoughts and emotions play just as important a role. A negative mind is like a veil that obstructs clear vision and prevents opportunities and grace from reaching us. On the other hand, positive thoughts about life, others, and ourselves reverberate grace back to us.

Let's say you see a woman passing by on the street who is overweight. The first thought that goes through your mind may be how overweight and unattractive you find her. Even though you never express that thought to her, the innate knowingness all around (her energy field) picks up its vibration. And, as is the law of cause and effect, it boomerangs back as a negative vibration to you. How can you turn that around? Well, the moment the judgmental thought enters your mind, quickly send the woman a blessing, wish her good health and the power to overcome her weight struggle (which surely they are going through), and tell her in your mind how beautiful she is. That way, instead of entertaining a negative thought that not only hurts the other person but returns back to you as a negative karma in your energy field, you have transformed it into grace by sending them positive thoughts and transforming your own mind.

Another example is someone who gossips about others. Even though the gossip is done behind others' backs and they may never know of it directly, a part of them—the wisdom of their energy field—will know. Remember, thoughts are waves, spoken words are waves, emotions are waves. They travel through space and time to reach their target, and the target will be impacted, as will the person who sent the wave. Thus our karma changes.

Some people, when they've been hurt, feel entitled to hurt their wrongdoer in return, an-eye-for-an-eye style. And others have the mind-set of, "I'm going to take care of me, even if it's going to hurt others." Both these types of thinking see the self as separate. To hurt someone who has hurt us only perpetuates the hurtful energy of the karma continuing forward. To think of oneself at the expense of another is to live in an attitude of selfishness. When we see the world around us negatively, our perception will plant a seed of such a cause that undoubtedly comes back negatively as well.

It's true that sometimes to survive one has to make a decision that ultimately may hurt another. However, the key in such moments is to act with love in the heart, not with a feeling of hate or revenge.

Just as our thoughts, as invisible as they may be, reverberate, so too do our emotions. Emotions are alive. Intense anger is like an arrow piercing its target's energy field. Hate is like throwing stones at its target's energy field. Fear makes people lie, cheat, and steal. Most emotions (those that are not positive) have their roots based in fear. Any intense thought or emotion will reach its target with greater force than a weak one, though both will reach and both will have an impact.

The emotions one feels within oneself can be compared to changes of the weather in the body. Just as the clouds may bring rain, so too, we feel sadness. Just as the winds may blow strongly, so too, we feel anxiety. Just as a wildfire may burn, so too, we feel anger. Just as the clouds may block the sun, so too, we feel down and depressed. Just as the sun may shine in a clear blue sky, so too, we feel happiness and joy. The more peace and stillness we feel within, the greater the likelihood of us feeling the same towards others, even when their actions might normally ignite a negative reaction.

As much as we may wish to blame circumstances, we are largely responsible for creating the obstacles that lie in our own life paths. Even if it's not necessarily specific actions that we are taking, the negative thoughts and feelings that we are radiating toward others or having about ourselves are throwing rocks on the road before us.

Let's consider the case of a lady in her early forties with a severe autoimmune disease. She attempted every alternative and traditional treatment to help overcome her condition; but one thing she never addressed throughout the process was the deep-rooted anger she held towards her sister, who had taken a large portion of her inheritance many years before and had always, in her opinion, made her feel inferior. Until the very end of the lady's life, that anger was stirring inside her. Unfortunately she was not able to survive the disease, nor heal the emotional wound before passing.

Emotions have tremendous power. No matter how much we may try to change our external circumstances, if we don't also address the more subtle levels of our being, our thoughts and emotions that have a direct impact on the chemistry of our body as well as our karma, we will feel stuck and blame our fate when we feel the effects of all the negativity coming back to us.

Writing Exercise

I want you to get a notebook to record the transformative journey you are about to begin. On the first page, write down the areas of your life where you feel stuck—where you have been wanting to change but have not been successful thus far. It might be your health or your weight. It might be your work or your finances. It might be your living location or situation. It might be your relationship, whether or not you are in one currently. It might be your inner growth and development.

13

Whatever aspect of your life that feels stuck, write it down. I have been asked whether there is a solution to all of our negative karma. My reply is that, to a large extent, we are creating our own karma. So, if it's not to our liking, we can undo and recreate or change the directions of the energy. Our actions, thoughts, and emotions from childhood until now have brought us to where we are. If we reverse some of the wrong choices we made unknowingly in the past, we can begin the process of changing our life's direction.

Some karma that we experience has been passed on from our ancestors. But even that, to some extent, can be transformed in the present and moving forward.

A small part of karma, however, cannot be changed. There are certain things that we are destined to experience and that we will find difficult. Of course, we cannot know which things fall into this category, so we have to keep trying and put in the effort anyway. It is important to note that our thoughts and emotions during such destined experiences still impact our karma. If our thoughts and emotions are positive during these times, despite the hardship, they create positive vibrations for unexpected changes down the line, in ways we could not predict.

Let's take the example of someone who is suffering tremendously from the loss of their job. They may have no savings and no potential job opportunities lined up, but if they go through this difficult phase with positive thoughts—free from anger at their ex-boss, working on their resume, and seeing the loss as an opportunity for something even better—the positive vibrations can change the course of their karma so that they encounter something better very soon. Life may throw a curveball at us that may be a result of our own past actions or our ancestors'; but how we respond to it determines the direction of that curveball and how it impacts the direction of our life.

Allow me to share some details from the life stories of some individuals who have opened up to me personally in order for me to help them create change.

A man in his fifties lost all his money to a business partner who deceived him. On top of that, his wife left him for another man. Both his business and his relationship were destroyed. Outwardly, he

15

was a very nice man, so I wondered what could have created such a karma for him. As I got to know him better, I realized he had a habit to twist the truth and lie, even about small things. After some time, I saw the tremendous amount of fear he carried inside. His intention was not to deceive anyone; lying was merely how he had learned to survive. His father had passed away a year before his tremendous financial loss and the end of his marriage. Since that time, he had not done any rituals in his father's honor, which was a common and important tradition in his culture. With him being his father's only son, the cultural ritual was considered even more critical.

These two factors—the lying and the neglect of ritual—were key to this man's painful karma. I asked him to make offerings for his father's life and passing, and I explained to him the consequences his lies were having in his life. The anger which the lies were fostering in the persons who were feeling deceived was creating scenarios of deception in his life, from his business partner deceiving him and running away with his money to his ex-wife cheating on him. Within four months after changing his unconscious habit of lying, along with following through with offerings for his father, the man started to earn money again and turned around his years of suffering.

Another case was a young girl who had attended college with the help of student loans. After having graduated, she decided to travel and default on her student loans. I explained to her that she had made a promise when she took out the loan. Even if she paid back only $100 a month, she could fulfill her responsibility. Her plan, though, would not only create problems with the bank and her credit; it would also influence her karma down the line. She was very resistant to listen, so, needless to say, things took a turn for the worse for her. Responsibility is a very important part of karma. This young woman wasn't ready to accept it and understand consequences. Every action has consequences, and we need to have long-term vision to see those when making choices and decisions.

The true power behind creating change in our karma is love. When love is there, there is also a sense of responsibility towards oneself, one's family, community, and the earth. Understanding responsibility is understanding the law of consequences, or of cause and effect. It is also knowing that the cause may not always stem from our actions, but also our thoughts and emotions, as well as the karma or actions of our ancestors.

The seeds of our visions cannot grow and thrive in a bed of weeds. Our negative karma has allowed those weeds to grow and the soil to become infertile. In order to nurture the soil's fertility, we need to clean up on many levels. This is the power we have to create change.

No matter what we want to achieve, we can never know if we will arrive there—even in the case of something as simple as going to the market to shop. We cannot know anything for a fact. But we can put forth the right effort toward that goal. Being empowered means knowing what the wrong efforts are, which create obstacles and make the journey more difficult, and what the right efforts are, which make the journey beautiful.

There are certain times in life when you have fallen so far due to circumstances that, even though you may want to change, you just don't have the willpower. Fatigue, sadness, and traumas can take a toll on your life. It's important to remember in such moments that even very small steps can start to turn the wheels of your karma in the right direction.

Writing Exercise

Write down in your notebook your intention to create positive change in your life. There is something about putting your visions on paper that creates more power and sends a direct message to the universe about your goal. It gets the ball rolling for internal and external shifts to happen toward your goal more easily. If you are lacking energy and inspiration to begin, just write down the simple fact that you want to create a change in your life for the better.

Now, let's begin the journey!

Chapter 2
Clutter and Karma

*"Every aspect of your life is anchored
energetically in your living space,
so clearing clutter can completely transform
your entire existence."*
— Karen Kingston

W hat does our home or workspace have to do with our karma? Well, a person's home is an extension of the person. Our environment impacts us. Not only does the tidiness aspect of our home or office impact us, but the specific objects or furniture in them carry certain energies, depending on where they were bought, what they mean to us, who the previous owner was (if they are secondhand) or who gave it to us. It takes a certain sensitivity to be aware of the subtle energies, but even a person who has little knowledge about the concept of energies knows when certain items make them feel better or worse. The clutter or lack thereof impacts our mind and emotions and the flow of our life by occupying space. A cluttered environment can lead to a cluttered mind. If you have to search a long time to find a particular pair of shoes, a shirt, or a photo, you probably have clutter. Most people enjoy walking into an upscale hotel room, and one of the main reasons for this is how clean and neat it is. It can sometimes feel sterile, yet also freeing on some level, to be in a clean environment.

Too often we collect more possessions than we need or use. We are given endless gifts for holidays, birthdays, and other occasions, and we stick them in a drawer not knowing what to do with them. We buy items because they are on sale. We put stuff in a closet or the garage and forget about it. All of these 'things' accumulate and before you know it, every closet, cupboard, drawer, under-bed space is full. We get used to holding onto things that take up space not only in the home but also, ultimately, in the mind. And because objects hold onto energies, they impact our energy and emotions as well. Some people like to buy used items that others previously owned. These objects carry the energies of the previous owner and, depending on the previous owner's disposition, could impact your energy field and recreate some of the same experiences for you. In other cases, people give gifts that are not fully from their heart or with ulterior motives, and thus the gifts carry those motives energetically as well. And then there are items we have received from people we love but with whom we have bad memories, and thus the object, unconsciously or consciously, reminds us of those painful memories. Perhaps it was a lover who was really attached to you, but you didn't feel the same way. They gave you a gift and, after your separation, they continued holding onto you in their mind. And perhaps now you are married but constantly having problems. The gift from that former lover in your home may seem harmless, but it carries the energies of your past and may somehow make you feel as if that person is still in your home. Obviously, this can cause many quarrels between a married couple. So, you see how subtle energies can be very powerful.

Go through your home. Take your time and start with one room. Keep thinking to simplify.

Start with a single closet or a cupboard in that room and look through it. Go through files, clothes, and collections of things. Start making a pile of things you can do without and keep adding to it. As you go through your belongings, ask yourself the following questions:

> ➤ Do I need it?
> ➤ Do I love it?
> ➤ Do I use it?
> ➤ Does it fit?
> ➤ Does it make me feel good?
> ➤ Who gave it to me? How do I feel about the giver and their intention?
> ➤ What energy do I feel from it?
> ➤ Could it be creating an interference in my life?

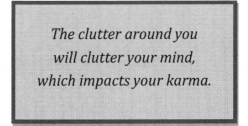

The clutter around you will clutter your mind, which impacts your karma.

Only keep things that you love, need, and feel good about, and release the rest. If you don't love or need it, it's just taking up space. And remember, the person who gave the item to us or who owned the item before us matters, because it carries that person's intention and energy. Continue with this process in every room of your house and in your office as well. Sometimes you can go through a room once and feel complete, only to have a second go at it at a later date to clear more things out. Do this in whatever way works best for you.

What are some of the things to look for? Many of us collect newspapers, magazines, or coupon books that are outdated, thinking that "one day" we will go through them or need them. Before you know it, five years have passed and they are just taking up room and turning yellow. If it's old, let it go, unless it has some specific value. And remember to recycle!

Books are very valuable, but if you don't like a certain book or will never read it again and have way too many other books that you don't enjoy, then go through your books and donate them to the library.

Then there are things that serve no other purpose than collecting dust. Perhaps we bought it or someone gave it to us many years back, and since then it has sat on the shelf. It has no real significance to us, but we don't like throwing it away either. Remember, objects don't necessarily have to be thrown in the trash, especially if you feel it can be valuable to someone else. You can donate it to a thrift store, give it as a gift to someone else if it looks like new, or put it by the trash bins for someone to take freely. But whatever you do, if it's not useful for you and you don't really 'love' it, let it go.

Some people love to hold onto photos. Nowadays in the digital age, it's easier to have many photos and have them take up only a very small space on a flash drive. But remember, just as objects carry energy, so do photos. If you are holding onto photos of past relationships, in some cases it could be interfering with your present relationship. Some partners are more sensitive to this issue than others. You need to be the judge of whether the photos carry good or bad memories, and whether they interfere with your relationship (if you are in one) or your life in general. People who are trying to get into a new relationship but are having difficulty need to examine whether they are holding onto the past by holding onto old photos, and whether doing so is interfering with their ability to move forward and meet a new partner.

If you have had bad memories with a person, better to get rid of items that are from them or remind you of them. And if it was a romantic relationship and the other person had a hard time letting go of you and possibly still holding onto you, its best to let go of their photo as well.

For some people, clothing is a big one, especially if they are in the habit of buying just because of sales. It's good to have ample clothing and shoes to fit the many occasions of life, but if you don't remember half of what you own, maybe it's time to let it go. Ask yourself:

- ➤ Does it fit you?
- ➤ Do you love it?
- ➤ When is the last time you wore it?
- ➤ Does the color look good on you?
- ➤ Does the style look good on you?
- ➤ Is it torn or does it need to be mended?

Sometimes we buy clothing just to have something to put on or because the design or color is appealing to us—but it may not actually look appealing on us. You want clothes to make you feel good and look good. If it doesn't fit you, you don't love it, and it doesn't enhance your appearance, let it go. If you haven't worn it in over a year, you probably never will. If it's torn and can be easily mended, then sew it and keep it, otherwise let it go. If it's hard to keep an objective viewpoint, then bring a friend you trust to give their honest opinion.

In your office or home, look through all the files, documents, and letters. Are you still holding onto love letters from someone of the past? Approach these the same way as with photos; decide whether you want to keep it or let it go and how it impacts your partner, if you are in a relationship. If you have papers from twenty years back, why are you keeping them? Throw away papers or bills that you don't need anymore. Go through your file cabinets at work and see what is necessary to keep and what is no longer needed. Think about creating space. Movement is hindered when there is little space. Energy, like a river, requires space to be able to flow. The clutter around you will clutter your mind, which impacts your karma.

Now, back to our discussion of gifts. Gifts can bring blessings to your life or can be like a curse. I once visited the house of a lady who had been through a tumultuous prior marriage. Even with her current husband, there were only fights and no peace. As I walked through the front door, two items caught my eye: a wooden statue and a wooden bowl, both decorative pieces. When I asked her about them, she mentioned they had been given to her by a man who had loved her in the past. This happened during the early days of her first marriage. This other man, despite knowing she was married, had given her these gifts and told her he wanted to be with her. Being young, she hadn't thought anything of it and accepted the gifts. When I explained to her the concept of energies and intentions, she was very skeptical. She was very attached to the two pieces and didn't think they could hold any power over her. Some time later, she separated from her second husband. The two items remained in her home.

It's good to realize sometimes how attached we are to certain things. Maybe what I was telling her was superstition, but the only way to find out would have been to remove the object for some time and see. She could have given it to someone who did not know the man and see if there was any change in her life as a result. She had had these items almost her entire adult life, and it took the loss of two marriages to finally consider the idea. She finally gave the items away and, though both her marriages were over, her relationship with her ex-husbands improved afterward.

In a similar story, there was a man who was separated from his wife but was having difficulty letting go of her. She was constantly asking him for money, but not filing for divorce or letting him go. Inside his house, I saw a white pot on the mantelpiece. It looked almost like an urn, and it had a curious energy. Standing on either the side of it were two statues, one of an African woman and another of an African man. This man himself was very hard-working, but it seemed that everything he did went sideways; it was like something was pulling the rug out from under his feet constantly. His wife, on the other hand, was a spendthrift who did not want to work during the entire time that they were married. She had bought these two statues. I asked him if he was willing to get rid of them. I felt they were binding him to her so that he could neither move on with his life nor have a proper relationship. It was obvious to me that the main connection that his wife saw with him was not a loving, sharing relationship but rather a bankroller whom she could use to her advantage. As soon as the man removed those items, their relationship shifted and his wife started to detach more. Finally he started getting offers for his business, and his finances started to take a turn for the better. You see how small objects, as insignificant as they may appear, can have a powerful impact on one's life.

Some people are naturally sensitive to energies and can automatically tell if an object feels off. Others are equally sensitive but, since they have had the object around for so long, they overlook it and require an objective person's help. Still others, though not sensitive, can develop this awareness of the nuances of energy but haven't done so yet. There's not a single person who does not notice the uncomfortable "vibe" when they walk into a room where people have just fought or something unsavory has just happened. Or, the exact opposite case—when they walk into a home and they feel the joy and happiness of its inhabitants. With objects, it's exactly the same idea.

As you examine your living and working spaces, you might become more aware of these energies and recognize what feels right and what doesn't. Make a pile of whatever doesn't feel right and then decide whether to get rid of it or not. And as you look at the gifts you were given, think about what intention the giver had, what your relationship with them was, and how you feel about them. If you feel the person cares about you and has good intentions for you, then their gift probably will reflect those intentions. Otherwise, if they are envious of you, gossiping about you, in competition with you, or don't wish for your happiness, then chances are their gifts are going to be a representation of that energy as well. Surround yourself with love and support.

It's easy to throw things into a drawer or closet and forget they exist. But in reality, not only are they still taking up space, but they are still bringing their own energy into your life. Just because something is stashed in your closet does not mean it's not impacting your life. Clutter is one thing; energy of objects is another. Start going through your drawers. If they are a mess, get rid of what you don't need. If your socks have holes in them, mend them or get rid of them. If you have singleton socks, get rid of them. Do the same for the things in your closets, cupboards, storage spaces, garage, basement, shelves, and under your bed. We may have many possessions that we think are "out of sight, out of mind," but they are very much creating an impact in your life and your ability to allow grace in. Get organized. As you organize your space, you organize your mind and the flow of your life.

What are some other things that don't get used in your space? If you have children, you probably have an abundance of toys. If your children have outgrown their toys or clothing, donate these things to someone who will. You might keep a couple for memories, but otherwise, they are just taking up space. All the clutter can also impact the children's' minds and their studies as well, which impacts their grades and the rest of their life and their karma.

It can be tempting to accept furniture, which are relatively expensive items—if someone offers a couch for free, for example. A couch is frequently used, and therefore it takes on the energies of the people in the home quite strongly. Be sure of whom you are accepting furniture from, their lifestyle, and their habits. If these attributes are positive, good. If not, then it would be better not to accept the couch. Though certain things can be cleansed of their negative impact and energetic accumulations, some are not worth the trouble, either because they are too small or their energy is just too heavy and convoluted. You want to bring things of joy and light into your life that support your mind and emotions to equally joyful and light.

After all your excess material possessions have been thrown away or donated, it is time to breathe and start organizing. If you often find yourself looking for things and can't find them, you probably need to set up an organizational system in your drawers, closet, cupboards, and file cabinets. Papers should be gathered together, as well as clothing, tools, computer stuff, and office supplies, respectively. I have been to some homes where loose photos, tweezers, a screwdriver, keychains, and jewelry are all kept in the same drawer. All that was missing was a piece of bread! And just as expected, not only could the inhabitant of that home never find anything; their life was in shambles, they juggled many things at once, and they were getting nowhere with their half-developed business plans. When you can see through your stuff, your mind can see through to make your visions a reality. Just as a river can't flow along its rightful path if there are many rocks, debris, and tree branches in the way, so too the river of grace and positive energy in one's life cannot flow. Getting rid of and organizing things lightens the load on your mind. Even though you may not consciously be aware of it, once your home or office is lighter, your mind will start working better. A clear mind makes clear decisions and the flow of such a person's karma goes in the direction that they dream.

Imagine a river. Its nature is to flow, just as your blood is meant to flow throughout your body. But branches fall, leaves fall, and they can block the flow of the river. It is the same with the body. When it is not functioning optimally, then blood, which is 70% water, becomes sluggish in its flow, as does the lymphatic system. Gradually, this accumulation becomes thick like phlegm. Likewise, if the flow of a river gets blocked for long periods of time, the water becomes murky and swamp-like with little movement. When we accumulate many things, the flow of energy in our home and office, and hence our life, is obstructed. Objects accumulating in excess create the same stagnation in your life.

So you've gotten rid of things. You've organized. What's next? Now is the time to dust and vacuum. Go into all the little corners and clear away the cobwebs. Clean the windows so that the light of the sun can shine into your life. Scrub the floors of all the old energy. Or, if you prefer, you can hire someone else to complete this phase of work. Cleaning is actually a very important thing to do when moving into a new home, even if it looks clean; you should clean it with the intention of clearing the previous owner's energies.

Now that the clutter is gone, it's time to fill your home with the energy of abundance and happiness. If you wish, you can bring in a professional feng shui practitioner to balance the energies of your home. One thing that I've found to always be supportive are jade plants. Having a live plant brings life to your home. However, be aware that plants also have specific energies based on their leaves. Those with harsh, pointing leaves can disrupt the energy inside the home. And of course, plants require care.

I hope you feel better inside your tidier home. These steps for de-cluttering may be difficult for some, especially if you have a habit of holding onto items. If you are one such person, it may be helpful to ask yourself why you need so many things. Do you really need them? Are they fulfilling a different role than their obvious purpose, such as filling the emptiness in your life? Do they make you feel abundant or important? Do they add to your sense of self? Do they give you a sense of false security? Do you live in scarcity and hold onto things out of fear? Do you keep gifted things so that you don't hurt the feelings of the giver? These are important questions to ask yourself in order to break the pattern of clutter so that, after all the work of clearing and cleaning, you don't fall back into similar habits.

When we clear our home of clutter, we are not only cleaning the place. Our home is where we spend a great amount of time; therefore, its state directly impacts our mind and emotions. Our mind and emotions are what bring about actions that set the direction of our karma. Oftentimes we forget how things are connected in our life and think of karma as some abstract term. We don't reflect deeply on what all the "causes" are and how their interrelation brings about the fruits of our life's journey.

Chapter 3
Your Body and Your Karma

"If anything is sacred, the human body is sacred."
— Walt Whitman

We often take our body for granted and separate the body's function from that of the mind and emotions. However, the body's functioning plays a critical role in our karma, not only through the illnesses we experience, but through our life in general. For example, when you feel fatigued, you may not have the energy to complete certain tasks nor have the clarity of mind to make the right decisions. When you have a headache, you may be quick to anger and snap at your boss or spouse, which can set in motion many karmic reactions. All of these are regular experiences as a human being. We all feel angry, tired, sad, and so on at certain times. But what we

39

don't realize is that our lifestyle and diet choices, and their effects on the body's functioning, can also be the precursor to the aforementioned negative emotions and mental states. If there is discord in the body, there is often discord in our life. If you have pain in your legs, you probably can't go very far when walking, as much as you may want to. It is the same with our visions and goals. If we have bodily discomfort, it means the natural flow of optimal functioning has been compromised and as a result the flow in our life has been as well. But it's not only when our body experiences physical ailments that the flow is compromised; it can already be compromised in subtler ways before it reaches a more chronic or even noticeable state.

Food and Drink

Food and drink have a direct impact on the mind and the emotions. There are several qualities of a food or drink to be aware of. Of course there is the nutritional content of the item, but there is also its "nature." For example, pepper has a warming nature. Cucumber has a cooling nature. Cheese has a phlegm-producing nature. Lemon has an astringent nature.

Eating the wrong foods, an excess of certain foods, or the wrong foods for your body type and condition can create adverse reactions within your body. For example, a person who has a tendency to get headaches may love spicy foods, yet this is exactly the wrong food for them: heat has a tendency to rise and is drying, and thus it could either be the cause of the headache for this individual or exacerbate the underlying problem.

When it comes to the nutritional value of foods, our body has a chemical balance it needs to maintain. It requires the building blocks and nutrients to do so. When we deplete our body of its requirements, we throw off this balance, which in turn can impact our emotions or thoughts. For example, if you are anemic due to a poor diet, your red blood cells are low. Your blood flow is generally weaker than the norm, though your entire body requires blood to bring nutrients to the cells and remove toxins. You may feel weak. Your mind may be less sharp. You may become forgetful. This can manifest a whole host of domino-falling reactions in the wheel of karma of your life.

Consider how eating the wrong combination of foods or drinking very little water can create constipation in a person. When there is constipation, the body is not able to rid itself of waste. Toxicity buildup in the body can have many long-term side effects. Think of the plumbing in your home, if food waste is thrown into the sink and the garbage disposal is broken. What kinds of smells would start to build up in your home? The body is the same. When there is stagnation in the digestive system, leading to an inability to rid itself of waste, it can reflect in a person's life, making it more stagnant as well. Letting go of waste from our food and drink is equivalent to letting go of thoughts and emotions that are no longer serving us. When we are constipated physically, things are stuck. And when we are holding onto our negative thoughts and emotions, the energies in our life cannot flow easily. Grace cannot flow. Opportunities cannot flow.

Food has a direct impact on our mind and emotions, and hence our actions and choices as well. If you eat too much sugar, it may make you hyper with energy in the moment, but then sluggish with a foggy mind a few hours later. If you need to study, the sugar may give you a helpful boost of energy, but it does not give you the best quality of mind.

Of course, some people have great resilience and it may seem that whatever they eat, they are functioning well. But what they are not aware of is that if they were eating better, they would out-perform themselves. They are also not aware of the long-term harm they are causing their body, which is not noticeable at the moment. Often we are short-sighted because the results of our actions are not immediately noticeable. Sometimes people tell me, "But I have been eating pepper all my life and I never had problems! Why now?" Or, "I have been eating cheese for decades! How come I have a problem with it now?" The answer in these cases is that it's only after some time, when our system has become weaker, that we feel the impact of our long-term choices. The same way that karma does not come back to us right away, the fruits of our poor dietary habits sometimes do not manifest themselves until many years later, when our body's ability to deal with the bad habits has reached its threshold.

Let's take another example. You may water your plant today. Tomorrow, you may not have to water it because the soil is still moist. Even after a few days, it may be fine not to water it, because there's still some moisture there (depending on the temperature and how much you watered it previously). After a week, the soil may be dry, but the plant's roots still have some water stored and so the plant appears to be doing fine. After fourteen days, the soil is dry, the roots are now drying out as well, and the plant has begun to look a little withered. And after twenty days, if the plant has still received no water, it begins to dry out and die. So it is with the body. You may be fine eating unhealthily for a certain period of time, until the body reaches its threshold and reacts. There may be subtle warning symptoms beforehand, but because you did not notice or chose not to do anything about those symptoms, then the apparent "sudden onset" of an issue surprises you. Again, every single decision we make and action we take has an effect. That is the law of karma.

Food is alive. It is what nourishes you and allows you to function. It has tremendous power over your mind, emotions, and life.

Unfortunately we are living in an age of processed foods. Anytime a food is not in its natural form (as it was grown), it will have a weakened life force, not to mention the preservatives added that can be harmful to the body, depending on their sources. That means that eating a banana versus eating candy is going to have quite a different impact on the body. Though they are both high in sugar, one is natural and easy to digest and the other is highly concentrated sugar, usually with artificial colorings. Additionally, the banana has more nutritional value than candy, which is nothing but sugar and stimulates a surge in energy temporarily without providing any additional benefits.

We talked earlier about how stagnation in the intestines can be a reflection of stagnation in our life as well. There are certain foods that are prone to causing stagnation in the body in the case of excessive consumption. For example, based on Chinese medicine, there are certain foods that are "phlegm"-producing foods. Such foods slow down the flow within our body. Foods that are either phlegm producing by nature or that create a lot of phlegm once digested (such as sugar, dairy, bread, short-grain white rice, alcohol, cookies, muffins, donuts, and so forth), if eaten in excess, can lead to sluggishness, resulting in fatigue and fogginess in the mind. A foggy mind is not functioning as sharply as it could otherwise. The decisions it makes are not always as rational as they could be.

Another food that can lead to stagnation is nuts and nut butters. Though nuts are healthy foods to consume, some people don't have the strength in their digestion to metabolize them effectively, especially if eating them in excess. In such cases they can be like glue in the intestinal lining, not allowing for proper absorption of nutrients or release of toxins.

Buildup of toxicity can be a result of waste not moving out of the body fast enough, but may also be due to other causes. Dairy cows are often given antibiotics and hormones while they are being raised. Whatever the animal is injected with or fed will go into the meat as well as the milk or products of that animal. Humans who consume any part of that animal will be consuming the antibiotics and hormones as well. Just as directly taking antibiotics can compromise the flora of the intestines, so can consuming meat or dairy products that have these added hormones or antibiotics injected into them.

Remember that anything that you put inside your body, whether it's drink, food, medication, supplement, or herb, will impact your body, your mind, and emotions. And the choices you make consequently create your karma.

Weight Management

Allow me to speak briefly about weight gain and loss, because it is an area of life where many feel they are a victim to their fate. It seems that everyone has been looking for the magic method to lose weight. There are hundreds of theories and some don't work at all, some are temporary, some are very strict, and some more gradual. But among all the weight loss methods that have been promulgated, rarely has over-toxicity of the body been spoken of. I delved into this issue in my prior book, *Lose Weight Unleash Your Creativity*. When the body is exposed to toxins and chemicals, one of the ways that the body tries to maintain its balance is by building a protection of fat around it, to keep the toxin latent so that it does not cause harm to the body. For example, certain heavy metals can be stored in fat cells as a way to protect our overall body from their harm. When we do a cleanse to release them, we may find that we also lose weight, not so much because of the certain diet, but because the fat no longer has to protect us from the toxicity and can be released from the body.

Another aspect of weight gain that you may have heard of already is that it can serve as an emotional protection. When we are overwhelmed by negative emotions that are difficult to face, we may have a tendency to eat to calm the emotions and in some ways make them latent as well. Instead of expressing the anger or frustration, we eat. Instead of feeling our sexual energy, we eat. Food puts a damper on the emotion, but of course it's not a real solution.

Your food choices are always key. Food becomes part of your cells and muscles and makes up who you are. Eating something that is whole is very different than eating something processed. Whole foods will be metabolized much better and will be a lot easier on your system. They will cleanse your body and give you better nutrients. All of this comes back to your karma. The choices you make affect your future. Those choices may seem difficult to make in the moment, but once you start to dig up the roots of the karma that is making it difficult to lose weight, for example, then changing the direction of your karma to match your desires will become more effortless.

Yet another key to weight loss is happiness. When we are happy, everything works better in our system; we digest better, our circulation is better, and we feel better. When we are unhappy, everything becomes more sluggish in our body and life.

Cleansing

At this point you have gained a general idea of how important the dietary maintenance of the body is to keeping a healthy mind and emotional state. And remember, a healthy mind, body, and emotional state adds to better choices and better karma. What we eat and drink is our medicine for healing our body, mind, and emotions. It becomes a part of who we are. The food and drink choices we make are critical in our well-being and the direction of our karma.

Now I want to talk about some basic steps to take toward cleansing and balancing the body. Some of them may seem very elementary, but unfortunately, it's the basic, simple things that are the most important, though we ironically tend to forget them.

Let's start with water. I have met so many people who drink very little water—and by very little, I mean only one or two glasses a day! I have found that there are usually four reasons that they drink so little. One, it doesn't taste good. Two, they forget. Three, they don't think it's very important. Four, they don't wish to have to go to the bathroom frequently.

Let me start by saying that 70% of your blood is water. Your blood needs to circulate and, if it's lacking water, it will become more sluggish and more toxins will build up in the system. The hydrogen and oxygen molecules of water are part of the metabolic processes of the body to bring nutrients to your cells and to remove toxins from your cells.

And it's clear that if we are not able to bring nutrients into our cells, we will become deficient in those nutrients and a multitude of illnesses will follow. In the same manner, if we are not able to remove toxins from the cells, then the buildup gradually leads to a multitude of illnesses as well.

Take constipation for example once more. Many people suffer from it, and one of the common reasons is not drinking enough water. Imagine your dishes after eating a meal. If you simply place them in your sink overnight, the remaining traces of food on the dishes will become dry and very hard to wash off. But after soaking the dishes in water, the food washes off quite easily. It is the same within the intestines. When you don't drink enough water, you can imagine how dry the intestines become, which makes it difficult for food waste to move through the system easily. Water and vegetables are two of the most critical ingredients to have good bowel movements, and good bowel movements are critical to cleanse the body. Therefore, water is critical in helping to balance and regulate the functioning of your body in general.

The next factor in cleansing the body is vegetables, as I mentioned above. So many of us have hated vegetables since we were young because we grew up eating processed foods. I used to be one of those people who got sick at the thought of eating broccoli. But life is all about habit. Just as we learn something, so can we unlearn it

51

and relearn a better habit. I would never have imagined that I would crave broccoli. But now that's the reality. Ice cream and sweets were my favorite food as a child. But now when I travel and have difficulty cooking and finding vegetables, my body now craves them desperately. Vegetables, apart from being incredibly rich in numerous nutrients, are like a broom that cleanse the body and help with regular bowel movements. It's important to have a large bowl of steamed mixed vegetables every day, and I emphasize the word "large." For most of us, if we have any vegetables at all, it's a small amount on the side or a few pieces in a salad.

But that's not what I am talking about. It's important to have a large bowl daily and to alternate the vegetables, having three or four different kinds each day, and not always the same ones. You can read more on this in my prior book, *Own Your Health Change Your Destiny.* Remember, the more regular your bowel movements, the more you are cleansing your body and letting go of toxins on a daily basis. The more you are cleansed physically, the clearer your mind will be and the more balanced your emotions. Eating vegetables adds a lot of important nutrients for the better functioning of your body in general.

> *Food has a direct impact on our mind and emotions, and hence our actions and choices as well.*

You can see from everything mentioned thus far in this chapter that a vital part of clearing karma is letting go of toxicity. The toxicity that builds up internally is one part of what impacts the mind to make wrong choices. When cleansing, it's always best to start with the colon, because that's the final pathway out of the body. Many make the mistake of starting with a liver cleanse, not realizing that their colon may not be fully evacuating waste. All a liver cleanse does in that case is start the cleansing process for the liver and cause the toxins to get backed up in the colon and reabsorbed into the system. Having one bowel movement a day, though good, does not mean the colon is not impacted and everything is functioning optimally. Many people can have waste not fully being released but still have daily bowel movements. Therefore, it's helpful when doing a cleanse to focus on the colon first.

A gentle approach to cleansing is better than an aggressive and rapid one that may backfire. For example, some people may do an aggressive cleanse for seven days by fasting from all food and drinking only water, but immediately following their fast, they may eat everything in sight without any control, thereby putting their body into a state of shock.[1]

Certain supplements can aid in the cleansing process temporarily to help in releasing toxins which have accumulated along the walls of the intestines over many years. Good-quality probiotics would be an important supplement to add for a few months as part of a cleanse. If you are uncertain about the best way to do a cleanse, it is advisable to get the support of a natural health care practitioner so you don't cause any harm to your body. Cleanses can be powerful, and it's important

---

[1] Please refer to my previously published book, *Own Your Health Change Your Destiny*, for a recommended gentle cleanse protocol.

not to overload the body and take supplements that may actually cause more harm. Not every person is the same; a supplement that is good for one person may not be good for you.

Many intestinal cleansing products that are sold over the counter have numerous herbs in them. Herbs are extremely potent—their power should not be underestimated. Not every cleanse product is suitable for everyone, as the constitution of the individual and their health history must be taken into consideration. It's best to have the support of your natural health care practitioner if you are uncertain what is best for you. Remember, food is medicine: for instance, chia seeds in a smoothie can support a beneficial increase in bowel movements. By changing your diet, you gradually start a cleansing process, incorporating more water and vegetables and removing many clogging foods, which most often are processed foods.

Body Products

What about all the body products we use such as shampoo, conditioner, soap, lotion, face masks, body oils, and makeup? Whatever is put on the body topically is absorbed and, in a way, is "food" for the skin. Many times we are fooled by labels that say "all-natural" or "pure" into believing the products to be safe. But those terms really don't have any real value; there are many chemicals in body products that can be harmful through long-term use. For example, simply using organic avocado oil as a skin moisturizer on your legs may be a substitute for the many other products that contain added preservatives and chemicals. Why not use something that is directly from nature and contains only one ingredient instead of something synthetically manufactured with preservatives and chemicals that potentially add to the toxicity levels in your body?

Just as foods can create stagnation and toxicity buildup in the body, so can body products with chemicals. Many products have synthetically derived scents that are harmful. It's important to note that scents directly impact the mind. Essential oils and scents are very powerful. They can impact the hormones and the chemistry of the brain directly. Be sure to use products with only organic essential oils for scents rather than chemically derived ones.

Some body products to be aware of are nail glue, nail polish, nail gel, hair gel, hairspray, moisturizer, sun tan lotion, facial toner, facial cleanser, face masks, makeup, shampoo and conditioner, and hair dye. Always remember, simplicity is best. The simpler the ingredients, the better. There are many products that are made from food or plant sources and are unaltered. They are less expensive, truly pure in their ingredients, and very simple. In the long term, these products will cause less damage to the body.

Breath

We breathe every day in order to stay alive, but rarely give it much importance or value. We take for granted that breath is life itself. Without breathing, we would die. When we breathe in, we bring in life and when we breathe out we release and let go of toxins. Often our breathing is very shallow and does not allow oxygen to be fully and deeply taken in. The less oxygen we allow into our body from shallow breathing, the more we allow toxins to build up.

Exercise is a great way to allow oxygen to circulate throughout the system. However, some people exercise so hard that their breathing becomes extremely shallow, especially during a cardio activity. Exercising in fresh air is even more effective than indoors. Simply taking a walk through nature can be very nourishing and cleansing on many levels.

Remember, breath is extremely powerful. With breath we can guide our intention and give it power and energy. For example, when you wish for something for yourself, through your breath and intention you can bring that wish to become more a part of your cells. You can allow it to become a part of you.

Breathing through our mouth and nose is not the only way we breathe. Our skin also breathes. One way to support this process is by doing body scrubs. There are scrub brushes that can be used in the shower to remove dead skin cells and refresh the body. Doing this once every couple of weeks can be helpful. Salt can also be used as a scrub. Both renew the skin cells by removing toxins and dead skin.

Sleep

Sleeping is something taken for granted until there is a lack of it; that's when you notice how much your mind is impacted. When deprived of sleep, you may become more short-tempered, lethargic, or foggy in the mind. You may feel a lot more emotional. It's at those times when you may say or do things that you don't actually mean and bring into motion a whole new set of negative karma. Imagine a person who has to work eighteen-hour shifts and has only five or six hours (or less) per day to sleep. Their body is under severe stress, their mind is tense and quick to react, and their emotions may be agitated and angry, even to the point of being volatile. As a result, they create a chain reaction of karma that can backfire on them. No matter whom or what we blame our circumstances on, karma is largely created as a result of our own actions and thoughts.

Resting and sleeping are very important factors of optimal physical health and weight. People think that losing excess fat is all about activity, but activity without resting does not allow the body to recover and thus weakens the body long term. Yin and Yang are very important aspects of life. At the core, the concept is balance. Yin is rest. Yang is activity. If you have too much of either, the other becomes off balance, kicking off an array of additional problems as well.

Since the mind is critical in making choices, falling asleep while watching TV will leave imprints on our mind that can impact the quality of our night's sleep, and hence our choices in life. It's best to not watch any TV at least one hour prior to going to bed. Let that hour be a time for reflection, for quietude, for peacefulness, for positive thoughts and recuperation from the day. Use that hour to send blessings to others, even those that have hurt you, and to be grateful for all that you have.

Drinking alcohol before bedtime is also not helpful, because it activates the liver. Many think that alcohol is very relaxing in the evening and see no harm in drinking a glass on a regular basis. Though it may initially have a relaxing effect, it will actually impact the quality of your sleep. Over time, insomnia can result from regular drinking in the evenings. The same drink that you thought was relaxing in the short term causes long-term stress because of the strain on the liver that is not allowing you to sleep deeply or at all. Hence, you are more stressed during the daytime and give a weaker performance.

Caring for yourself is caring for the gift that you have been given—your life. Self-care does not have to be an egocentric pursuit, but rather should be a sacred one. When you love and care for yourself, your mind becomes more positive and you can see more beauty around you. When you see more beauty around, chances are you will treat the world better as well.

Sometimes we need an extra boost to become balanced. Interacting with life and our environment can throw our energy off balance, and as a result we may act in ways we would not if we had less stress and more peace within. If you do things for yourself that make you feel more positive and relaxed and that purify your mind, the better your choices will be and the more balanced your mind and emotions will be. And, as a result, the more selfless and kind your actions will be—as you slowly transform your karma to produce the fruits that you desire.

Basically, anything that creates tension in your life over a period of time will impact your mind, emotions, and physical body. Negative thoughts and emotions have a greater tendency to surface under such circumstances and result in actions that create negative karma. Therefore, taking care of yourself and understanding the importance of a healthy body and its relationship with the mind and emotions is key to causing a change in your karma. The more at peace you feel, the higher the chances that you will create more peace in your life. If things are not going your way, it's not just your bad luck; to a large degree, you actively play a role in changing it. That's why you need to understand the factors that are impacting your life and its direction.

Chapter 4
Making Amends to Change Karma

"Study the past if you would define the future."
— Confucius

As much as we try to live in the present, our past follows us through our karma and leads us in various directions. The wheels we have previously set into motion and the energetic patterns of our past continue to impact our present. At times, when we feel like a feather being blown by the wind, it's actually the wind of karma that is directing us. How we impact others, whether positively or negatively, reverberates back to us. It can come back within an hour or it can come back after years. The resentment others carry in their hearts as a result of our wrongful

63

actions or words can be like a curse in our lives, creating constant battles that seem to never end. In the moments of our reactions towards others, we may feel entitled to be angry, to abuse, to lie, to cheat, to say hurtful things, but the stains of pain, hate, and anger which these reactions leave behind can be extremely difficult to remove. We may feel we are free and clear after our outburst, but the pain we have caused the other person remains with them, and any thoughts they have about us will most likely be negative. Those who are deeply hurt by us send constant hurtful energies back to us subconsciously, due to the suffering they experience as a result of our harshness. It's the law of cause and effect. What is sent forth comes back. Sometimes it takes less time, sometimes more. But it most definitely returns, because that is the law of energy, the law of life. The visible and invisible worlds are intertwined.

Our actions which hurt someone else block the flow of grace into our life. Likewise, any pain we carry within ourselves as a result of others' actions blocks the flow of grace. Ultimately, the negative repercussions of pain others suffered at our hands are like a mirror that deflects positive energy from reaching us. And the pain we carry within can be like a wall that prevents the light of grace to enter us. Grace comes as a result of love, and being in a state of peace and love allows for openness, receptivity, and flow. The question is, how do we remove the karmic impact of our past actions towards others and the pain that we hold within ourselves as a result of others' actions? That is something that we will go into fully in this chapter.

An important point to mention here (though it arose also in a previous chapter) is that our karma is not only a result of our own deeds but also those of our family. We are not islands. Whatever karma our family members create will ultimately impact our lives.

Let's say a husband leaves work very angry at his boss and drives incredibly fast through the streets to release his frustration. On the way, he hits another car and the other person is seriously injured. Now he has to pay a huge sum of money to that person, is himself injured, and cannot work for some time. His wife, who is a stay-at-home mom, is left with no income to support herself and their three children. Yes, it's the husband who won't be earning any money for some time, but the rest of his family has to suffer along with him.

Another example is a woman who has no control over what she eats and consequently gains a substantial amount of weight. Her knees and back are always hurting. She has frequent debilitating headaches and high blood pressure. And suddenly, at the age of forty-five, she ends up in the hospital with a heart attack. She may survive the heart attack and come back home. She may need heart surgery to save her life. But the pain she has to go through—worrying about her well-being, going to and staying at the hospital, paying the hospital bills—is not a burden that she carries alone; her husband and children carry it as well. Weight loss it not just about appearances. It's about being healthy and responsible.

So, it's very clear that whatever action we take to counteract the long-term impact of our own lack of responsibility will backfire on us as well as our loved ones, in direct or indirect ways. Often we are not thinking about consequences when we say, do, or think things. It takes self-reflection to become aware of the repercussions. It helps to ask ourselves the following questions in order to differentiate between constructive or destructive actions, thoughts, or words.

> ➢ How will the other person feel as a result of what I do?

> ➢ Will the other person be hurt by what I do?

> ➢ Is my decision to act based in anger or love?

> ➢ Am I taking my family into consideration when I am making the decision to do a specific action?

> ➢ Will I be happy with myself after this action?

We tend to remember wrongdoings which have been done to us many years later. The scar that is left behind does not heal quickly. Yelling, stealing, being angry, hitting, and lying to someone are not benign actions. Sometimes we think of stealing as something that is typically done to a stranger—for example, a person stealing a computer from a store. But stealing can also be taking your sibling's share of inheritance and feeling you are entitled to it, or stealing money from your spouse out of anger during a divorce. The pain it leaves behind has deep roots, and unless we support the other person to transform that pain and heal the wound we caused, it may never go away and, as a result, the karma of it continues to send its ripples back to us.

Many indigenous cultures speak about karma and what they do to alter it. In Bolivia, the indigenous people speak about karma as one's "luck." If you go to see a shaman and they read the coca leaves to tell you about your future, they refer to it as "looking at your luck." And if what they see is not positive, they offer to perform rituals to "change your luck." In other words, they do not see karma as fixed but as something that can be changed. And they see karma as a result of your actions thus far, which have created your "luck." For the shamans of South America, nature is alive and all of the elements have a spirit within them, and we as humans are always in relation with nature and the universe. Nature's energies play a very important part in transforming our personal karma, if we know how to work with it. By burning offerings in fire, or giving offerings to the ocean or to the earth, or doing cleanses in rivers, these rituals connect your energy to nature to allow for a transformation of your luck, or your karma.

The world around us is alive and responsive to us. It's unfortunate that we live our lives with the greatest healer all around us—nature—and fail to interact with it for the most part. Healing happens in the invisible world, and learning to have a relationship with that world is what helps our transformation.

We have all lived our lives unknowingly hurting others and also being hurt by others. We have seen our reactions to being hurt, and others' towards us, as natural. That does not mean that those actions have not left their marks in our paths of karma. But now that we are more conscious that we can play a role in changing the direction of our karma, we are able to take steps towards doing so.

Writing Exercise

We have all made mistakes in our lives. We have done things, said things, and felt things that we are not happy about in hindsight. On a new page in your notebook, make a list of all the people, alive and dead, that you feel you may have hurt. Next to their name, add the specific thing that you did that you either regret or feel could have hurt them. Some things are easier to acknowledge.

Some things we prefer to forget. But even if we prefer to forget the hurtful action or word, it continues lurking deep inside as something we know wasn't right. Did we lie to someone out of fear? Did we scream at someone because we were frustrated? Did we take another woman's husband away from her? Did we take another man's wife away from him? Did we steal money from our business partner? Did we hit someone in anger? Did we gossip behind someone's back? Did we make someone feel small in front of another and embarrass them? Did we deceive someone for our own benefit? How many men have your hurt? How many women have you hurt? How many children have you hurt? The list can go on and on.

It's important to be honest with ourselves. We are doing this within the privacy of our hearts. It is between us and the universe, between us and God, between us and our own inner soul. But we need to take others' hearts into consideration in all our actions.

Keep this list in the back of your mind for now and we will go into how to transform the karmic energy a little bit later.

Writing Exercise

Now, make a list of all the names that come to mind of people who have hurt you, alive or dead. If you remember the hurt, it's significant enough to write down. Don't try to justify anything or brush it off as being small. If it's in your heart and mind, it has left a mark. Some things may have left a mark but you don't remember them at the moment. Don't worry. As you work through this book and the layers are cleared, you will remember. You can come back and finish these exercises later.

Take the list and write out specifically what those people did that really hurt you.

The negative emotions that you feel toward people who have hurt you create barriers which prevent grace from flowing into your life. Remember that when someone hurts another person, nine out of ten times it is unintentional; and those who act intentionally are lacking awareness and act out of ignorance. Anytime someone does something to hurt us intentionally or unintentionally, it's a cry for compassion on a much deeper level. They are hurting inside and as a result they hurt another, even if they cannot admit it. It's important for you to not create a rebounding karma by hurting them back, but rather to create a more positive karma for yourself by transforming the pain. I have heard people say it's better to avoid negative people; but I believe that those who are negative are suffering inside and, rather than being avoided, are in need of more love. If you are strong enough within yourself, try to show more love, or at the very least stay neutral, when confronted with negativity. If you find you are not in a place to handle another person's suffering and negativity, then you must deal with your own suffering first before your container has the space for the suffering of another. In such a situation it may be better to avoid the person, but with love, until you feel you can have compassion for them.

Writing Exercise

We experience numerous endings in our romantic relationships and friendships throughout our lives, whether through divorce or separation of some kind. These endings leave behind bitter memories which may continue to haunt us in the present. In your notebook, make a list of all such endings.

> *To do an action with love*
> *and to offer our time on*
> *behalf of another is a*
> *priceless gift.*

Writing Exercise

Miscarriages and abortions are also a loss of a relationship and can cause tremendous pain to the parents. Write down any miscarriages and/or abortions you have had (this applies to both men and women).

We have now created a list of many painful experiences, both those that we have been the receivers of and those we have caused others. Now it's time to make amends to begin the process of transforming the energy and our karma. As I mentioned earlier, nature is the greatest healer. The indigenous cultures would regularly give offerings to the earth, the river, and the ocean, as a gesture of respect and gratitude. This same gesture can also be done on behalf of the pain we have caused another or the pain we feel as a result of another's action, no matter whether it was done intentionally or not. Each offering must be done with a deliberate intention coming from the heart, not mechanically. An offering can take numerous forms. Here are some examples:

- ➢ If there is a prayer that is part of your spiritual practice or religion, offer that prayer for the person.

- ➢ If you have a practice of praying with a rosary (prayer beads), no matter what your religion or spiritual path, spend thirty minutes doing prayers on behalf of the person you have hurt or who has hurt you. Set aside a certain number of rounds on the prayer beads dedicated to that person.

- ➢ Buy food and give it as an offering to a poor person on behalf of that person.

- ➢ Buy sweets and give it as an offering in your church or temple on behalf of that person.

- ➢ Buy a gift for the poor and give it on behalf of that person.

- ➢ Buy seeds and place to feed the birds on behalf of that person. Do this for several days or weeks.

- ➢ Water a dry plant in the park on behalf of that person.

➢ Light a candle and offer your prayers for that person.

➢ Ask your heart what you could do to heal this karma, and listen to what your heart tells you.

Remember, no matter which type of offering you feel is right, do it with all your heart and make sure you take at least half an hour of your time for each person and incident. Time and love are the most precious gifts that we have to give. To do an action with love and to offer our time on behalf of another is a priceless gift.

As you do the offerings, which may take weeks or months, you may remember more people you have hurt or who have hurt you. Add them to your lists and continue with your offerings.

You may notice after starting the rituals to heal your karma that you feel gradually lighter after each one that you complete. You may also gradually notice many things that were stuck in your life start to shift and many paths opening up for you.

When it comes to relationships that have ended, we often separate from the person but we don't let go of the pain or the physical items (gifts or belongings) from the relationship. All these items still carry that person's energy, and if the memory is negative, you are maintaining a connection with that energy, which ultimately is not supportive for your life.

Look at the list of people that you have separated from. It's necessary to do a ritual of completion for these ended relationships. Just as there are rituals for birthdays, funerals, marriages, and divorces, it's important to find closure energetically as well with the concerned individuals themselves. Even if there are negative memories—maybe especially if there are such memories—it's important to do a ritual and give an offering on behalf of the person, such as I listed above. If you are still holding onto an item that such a person gave you and it represents bad memories for you, you can do a ritual of releasing it and giving it away, followed by cleansing your home. Examine your home and let go anything that you see that is a gift from a broken relationship and that brings back bad memories. It's not about letting it go with hate and anger, but letting it go with prayers and compassion. If more memories come to mind as a result of the release of the objects, do offerings once again on behalf of the person. Continue to do rituals on behalf of the person until you feel complete within yourself and you arrive at a state of love and peace in relation to that person.

For some, abortions and miscarriages leave behind traumatic scars. For those who wanted a baby and lost it through a miscarriage, there's a deep sadness. For those who aborted for whatever reason, though circumstances may have compelled them to make that choice, they may still suffer from having done so. Either way, there is an ending that took place, and just like any other ending, it needs a ritual of acknowledgement and prayers. As shared before, flowers and prayers can be offered on the child's behalf. You can also give offerings to the earth. Listen to your heart and follow what feels appropriate. Give them the respect and gift of time and prayers. Allow any grieving that has been locked up to flow.

And if you wish, you may want to adopt a child into your family, or help a child who is living in poverty or in an orphanage by simply paying for their schooling or food.

And finally, the last type of separation is the one that comes through death—death of our loved ones and our ancestors. Unfortunately, in most cultures, the only ritual that is done on behalf of those who have passed away is performed directly when the person has passed away, and nothing more. They become "out of sight, out of mind" and forgotten soon thereafter. Our ancestors play an incredibly important role in our life, whether we have known them or not. Their energy is connected to us. It is because of our ancestors that we are here and the karma that they have created, to lesser or greater degree, impact our own karma and the direction of our lives. Our ancestors are an extension of our lives, and it is crucial to continue to offer respect to them long after they are gone. Their karma is like ripples that blend into our own energy and karma. Giving offerings on their behalf ultimately comes back to us as tremendous blessings, gradually releasing the ripples of any negative karma from our lives. Our prayers and offerings are valuable to their spirits long after they are gone, because an energy matrix of theirs continues to remain. It doesn't matter if you believe in reincarnation or heaven and hell, or have any other religious or spiritual beliefs regarding afterlife. We are a continuation of our ancestors, and prayers and offerings done on their behalf lift the vibration of our ancestral lineage, including ourselves. Ideally, it is best to honor them at least once a year. You can even dedicate an area of your home to your ancestors, placing their pictures in a specific area of the home to invoke their blessings.

Take a moment and reflect on your ancestors who have passed during your lifetime. Have you done anything on their behalf other than attending their funerals? Some of us may not even have done that. It doesn't matter how long ago they passed; it's important for you to do an offering on their behalf. If you are still carrying resentment about something they did, do an offering to release the pain and free yourself and their spirit. You can light a candle, buy flowers, do prayers with their picture at home, or go somewhere in nature and offer water, flowers, seeds for the birds by the roots of a tree on their behalf. By honoring them, you are opening yourself to more grace.

Making amends by doing offerings for transforming karma does not end there, though. Our lineage impacts our karma, but our living family is our present line of connection impacting our karma. Anything one family member does not only affects their own life and karma but that of the rest of the family as well. Taking care of our health is not just an individual affair, but a family affair. Making responsible decisions is a family affair. Sometimes one family member is more aware than the others and in this case, if it's you (after all, you have picked up this book and are reading it), then you can also do offerings on behalf of your living family members to help shift their karma, or at the very least awaken them from their ignorance and heal their pain. Every person should take responsibility for their karma and how their karma impacts others, but when a person has not reached that level of awareness yet, you can do prayers and offerings on their behalf for the mistakes they are making. Just as your offerings and prayers lift the vibration of your ancestors, so too do they lift that of the family members alive around you.

If your spouse drinks to excess often, yells at you, or is abusive, you can do offerings on their behalf to help them heal the pain that has led them to such behavior—whether you choose to stay in the relationship or not. It may be hard to have compassion in those moments, but try to come to your heart, release your pain, and separate yourself enough to see them and their pain objectively.

Writing Exercise

Write down a list of the actions that your child, spouse, or parent does that is always causing distress in your life, others' lives, or even their own life. Once a year, reflect on things that have occurred within your family, especially the bad incidents, and make offerings.

It's important as a family to do offerings on each other's behalf and to support each other through prayers. Just as one person's anger, whether expressed or held inside, sends ripples to another person, so too prayers and offerings of love lift the vibration of the other.

Let's say your son hit another child in school. It will be a karma that he is creating in his life, even at such a young age. And you as a parent can do offerings on his behalf both for your son to heal his anger and for the child that was hit to make amends.

You can even set aside five minutes every day and do prayers and offerings on their behalf. Or, once a week you can leave seeds for the birds on their behalf with prayers, give gifts to the poor, or give offerings to the earth. Whatever you choose to do, remember that the universe is alive and aware and your offerings will be registered.

In the same way that nature is alive and supports you in healing your karma, so too it registers your respect for it. We are all alive because of nature. If the sun did not shine, the rains did not come, the seeds of the abundance of food that feeds us would not grow. If the trees did not exist, we would not be able to breathe. We are here because nature supports us. Every part of nature is sacred and we must respect all of it. How we treat nature also ripples back into our lives. The trash that we throw on the beach often gets washed into the ocean and unknowingly entangles a fish or other sea life, causing its death. Indirectly we are killing life and not taking care of the earth. We are responsible for the pollution that we produce. We need to walk with more mindfulness and appreciation for all of life, even small flies and spiders, not to mention cows and birds and all other animals. Every part of nature strives to live and survive. Even a fly's life matters. We may kill a fly, thinking of it as insignificant, but that fly came from a family. Its life and family may not seem important to us, but that thought lacks humility.

Once we become more sensitive to nature and its energies, we begin to understand that the fly suffers just the same as a human does.

Allow me to share an interesting story. Many years ago, I went camping with a group of friends, around twenty people in all. We found there were many ants and small spiders in our campground. We were in the woods, after all— their natural habitat. Generally, in my life, I do not kill even the smallest bug. If I see a spider in my home, I put it into a cup and release it outdoors. During this camping trip, everyone except two of us was getting bitten by the ants and spiders. Interestingly, we were the only two who followed the practice of not killing any living things. Later on I was told by a shaman that the animal kingdom is connected; when you have a tendency to kill spiders in your home, the spiders elsewhere know whether you are their protector or not. The innate wisdom of nature! All animals know who have killed their ancestors.

Writing Exercise

In your notebook, recount all of the times you may have killed any living thing, whether it's a fly, a spider, an ant, or a bird. Maybe you were driving too fast and hit an animal by accident. List all incidents. In the same way you did offerings for people who have hurt you and whom you have hurt, make offerings on behalf of those animals and nature for unknowingly having hurt them.

Chapter 5
Thoughts, Emotions, and Karma

"The question is not what you look at,
but what you see."
— Henry David Thoreau

Though only the physical body is visible, we are made of energy. The physical body itself is composed of a denser form of energy; however, surrounding our body is a subtler form that is not visible to the physical eye, yet extremely powerful and palpable nonetheless. The concept of an energy field may be familiar to some but new to others. For those for whom it's a foreign idea, I want you to think of how frequently you may have met someone or entered a room and immediately felt either a pleasant or unpleasant sensation, which had nothing to do with the words spoken by the person or the appearance of the room or any other obvious factor. For example, perhaps meeting with one person made you very uneasy and tense, yet another made you feel happy and inspired, both without any conversation exchange. The reason for experiencing these sensations is the energy field of the person or room. The entire world is made up of energy in various levels of vibration. There is no judgment inherent in the energy as to whether a person is good or bad; ultimately it's about the frequency, or vibration, of the energy.

An energy field expands beyond our physical body, surrounding us in an egg- shaped space. Along the body are energy pathways, which are known as meridians in traditional Chinese medicine, and along the center of the body we have what are known as chakras.[2]

These meridians run along the entire body from head to toe on both the front and back. There are twelve main meridians, and they are related to organs or organ systems within Chinese medicine.

[2] For more comprehensive information on chakras, please refer to *Wheels of Life: A User's Guide to the Chakra System*, a wonderfully informative book by Anodea Judith.

Each meridian also has a certain number of points along it, which are the points used for treatment in acupuncture. The acupuncture points along the pathways stimulate a specific function within the body. The same way that a specific switch will turn on a corresponding light in the bedroom, a specific acupuncture point will perform its specific function. Let's say that a person is experiencing pain. By stimulating the necessary acupuncture point, one can bring flow and balance to the respective area of the person's body and reduce their pain. So, by stimulating the energy point for a certain function, one can cause an improvement in the function of the physical body.[3]

According to Chinese medicine, all emotions are related to specific organs. When a person experiences a certain emotion frequently, it can weaken the functioning of that organ. For example, too much fear can weaken the kidneys' energetics. Too much anger can put a strain on the liver's energetics. Too much sadness can weaken the

---

[3] For more information on meridians as relates to Chinese acupuncture, please refer to *Chinese Acupuncture and Moxibustion* by Cheng Xinnong, Liangyue Deng, and Cheng Xinnong.

lungs' energetics. What that means is that not only is an organ itself compromised in its function, but the pathway along the body related to that organ becomes compromised in its flow, even prior to the organ's functioning being affected.

The experiences that we have in life provoke thoughts and emotions that directly impact the pathways and organs of our body, either enhancing flow or blocking it. When there is a blockage in the energy flow of the body, it will naturally impact the flow in one's life as well. Imagine being in pain. Your thoughts and emotions under such circumstances will be constricted. Your ability to accomplish certain things will be compromised. You may be quick to anger because of it. All of these are repercussions of the blockage in flow, which in turn will impact the way you respond to the present and create the karma of your future. Hence, the thoughts and emotions that we have directly impact the fruits of our future life experiences and karma.

Chakras, on the other hand, are the seven energy centers that run along the central line of the body, both on the front and the back. They have certain qualities attributed to them and, if they become stagnant, so do those qualities. For example, the chakra center located on the throat supports our speech and expression. If this area becomes blocked, then our ability to express ourselves becomes blocked as well. This explanation over-simplifies their power, but at the very least it communicates the idea that we are more than just a physical body. Though it is important for all chakras to be clear, I have found the heart chakra, located in the center of the chest, to be of special significance when it comes to our karma. When this center is clear, the doorway of love and compassion is open. With that, grace flows into one's life even more powerfully. It is not to say that the other six centers are not important, but that this center sets the stage for many experiences of life. When it is clear and open, so is the door to more magic in one's life.

Anytime there is a blockage in any channel or chakra, or in our energy field, there will be consequences of some kind in one's life. Some of these consequences may be minor at first but become something major later on if left unaddressed. These blockages directly impact our thoughts and emotions in the same way that our thoughts and emotions can be the cause of blockages in our life.

Our thoughts and emotions are pure vibrations and, as such, they are fluid and have the capacity to impact their surroundings. The external stimuli from the world impact our thoughts and emotions, hence the vibrations that we send out. Even in the womb, these vibrations begin to form in us as our parents' thoughts and emotions, as well as the sounds and vibrations of the external environment, interweave with our development. This interweaving goes back to our ancestors. One can say that the vibrations that form our thoughts and emotions are partially inherited from our ancestors. As we grow, our experiences continue to stimulate our senses and leave imprints, changing or deepening the patterns we have developed that make up our thoughts and emotions.

What do our thoughts and emotions have to do with our karma? Well, any action we take is preceded by a thought or an emotion. Even if we never take action, our thoughts and emotions travel, since they are ultimately vibrations. How is it that your friend calls you just a minute after you think about her? How is it that you feel your son is in danger at a given moment even though you have not spoken with him? How is it that you know your sister needs you, without her saying something? Because the vibrations of thoughts and emotions travel through time and space.

Experiences evoke thoughts and emotions within us. When a specific stimulus is more frequent or more intense, it has a greater tendency to leave an imprint within our energy to have a certain thought or emotion more frequently or intensely. For example, the habit of continuously watching horror movies will constantly stimulate the emotion of fear in you, whether you are aware of it or not. It will create tension in the body. Continuous stimulation of fear will eventually leave imprints in our energy field that makes us view the world in a more fearful way and react to the world in such a manner. All of our thoughts, emotions, and interactions, especially if they are more frequent, leave an imprint that will have consequences in our life choices and ultimately create our karma.

> *Our thoughts and emotions are pure vibrations and, as such, they are fluid and have the capacity to impact their surroundings.*

When experiences are more difficult or emotions are such that create tension in our body, the flow within our body gradually becomes blocked, as well as the flow of grace into our life. The more imprints we accumulate in our own energy, the more we project the same out into the world, hence changing the direction of our karma.

Let's take the example of being in a home environment where there is a lot of violence and anger. The presence of such things around us will create tension in our body that blocks the energy flow, in addition to leaving imprints of violence and anger in our mind and impacting our vision of life. Anger leaves repercussions of negative energy both for the recipient and for the one experiencing it. It's like a fire that burns the harmony between two people leaving only ashes behind. The traumatic energy that it leaves behind is the karma that it creates in our life.

When we learn to regard emotions and thoughts as energy forces with tremendous power, we can understand why, in many instances, we used to be ignorant as to why our karma is the way it is. We never considered that those were the factors changing the direction of our karma.

Whatever we expose ourselves to, whether real life experiences or movies, are powerful in leaving imprints behind that impact our mind and emotions, which in turn can direct the choices that we make in life. Experiences are vibrations that impact our own vibrations. Our thoughts and emotions are vibrations that impact the world around us and our karma.

Thoughts have great power over our karma. They are alive as energy. Remember that the nature of thoughts is energy, and the waves of energy pass across time and space to reach their source. Whether the person we're thinking about is still alive or has passed away, our thoughts flow to their recipient and boomerang back to us. Bad thoughts towards the world come back to us as what can feel like a curse. Good thoughts towards the world come back to us as grace. Negative thoughts create separation between you and grace like clouds preventing the sunlight from shining through. You might also compare having negative thoughts to sitting in a car whose engine won't start or which is driving in a direction that you don't want to go. Either way, it's keeping you stuck.

If you were to close your eyes and imagine what it feels like in your body to have a negative thought versus a positive one, you would quickly notice how the negative thought makes you tenser whereas the positive thought opens you up and relax you. Positive thoughts align you with love, which is grace—which is karma as you wish it to be.

It doesn't matter if the person receiving your thought is close or far away; energy travels. Thoughts are the precursor to action. Often we confuse action as the sole creator of karma, but thoughts are the subtle form of action. Of course, stealing something and thinking about stealing something are not the same. In such cases, the thought is about taking an action or not taking an action. However, even thinking about this type of action creates negativity in our energy because it's a selfish thought that does not take into consideration the impact of harming others. An increase in such thoughts would only reinforce the negativity. Thoughts are the subtler form of a slap in the face if they are negative. In contrast, imagine having thoughts such as, *what can I do to help this person?* Such thoughts open the heart and create more compassion within your energy. Even if you never actually do anything to help the person, the fact that you are on the track of helping another (rather than harming them) changes your vibration to one of love and opens you to grace.

When a person enters our line of sight, we have a tendency to automatically have a thought about them. That thought, even if left unexpressed, is like an arrow to the target. Let's say you walk past a man who carries some extra weight on his body. The first thought that comes to your mind may be about his excessive weight and his appearance. That is a negative thought. You might justify it as being a fact, but nevertheless, it's a thought of judgment and it sends an arrow out that ultimately returns to you. Now imagine that the next time you walk past a person who carries extra weight, you have the same thought but you immediately catch yourself. Even if the arrow has already been sent by the initial thought, you quickly add the thought, *You are beautiful. God bless you to care more for yourself.*

We have the ability to turn each negative thought into a prayer or a positive affirmation towards other people. We have learned to do affirmations for the negative thoughts that we have about ourselves to try to manifest better things in our life; now let's take it to the next level by sending positive thoughts towards others about whom we have negative thoughts. It's in this manner that we start to turn the karma of negative thoughts to positive prayers and positive karma: by sending blessings to others. We can transform the painful arrow of negative thought into the golden light of grace and blessings.

Therefore, it's important to watch not only the thoughts that we have about ourselves and our lives, but also the thoughts that we have about others, especially those that may push our buttons or trigger our negative thoughts and emotions. Many of us have had an experience with a family member that has been extremely hurtful and we have never forgotten it. We may go through life never speaking to them, with all the hate and anger cooped up inside and being directed toward them every time we think about them. The same could be true with friends, coworkers, or acquaintances. The energy of the feelings and hurtful thoughts ultimately hurts us because it creates blockages within us. It also returns to us directly, because the law of life is cause and effect. We may feel completely justified in our feelings about some harm that's been done to us, and if their action was out of greed, hate or anger, the wrongdoer will reap their own karma. However, we need to take care of our own reactions that ultimately create our karma.

Transform everything bad that you might say about another person to something positive. Transform any negative thought you have about another person to a prayer of blessings. This is where many people who feel they are not "doing" anything negative wonder why negative things are happening to them. They are not aware of their own negative thoughts and emotions, which are the subtler forms of actions, constantly being sent to others. So, by transforming your negative thoughts and emotions about others to prayers and blessings, you start the process of clearing the karma that is leading your life in the wrong direction.

Negative self-talk has the same impact for our karma. Imagine that you are running a race and someone in the stands screams, "Go, go, go. You can do it!" while another screams, "Stop! You will never make it. What's the point?" How would you respond to the second person? Some of us have a thick skin and may not be affected as much. But most would become weakened by the second voice if they heard it enough times. Now imagine that someone in your head is doing that to you all the time. You wouldn't be able to get very far in life, right? With a negative voice in our head, we harm ourselves and close the channel of grace. If you tend to have self-directed negative thoughts, there is probably someone else in your family who has similar thoughts about themselves. It could be an energy that has been passed down through the ancestral line, and it may be the reason why it's so difficult to turn the thought into a positive one within yourself.

Having negative thoughts about others, even if they are never said aloud, will impact them as well and return to us down the line.

Writing Exercise

Take out your notebook. Write down all of the negative thoughts that you have about yourself. Some of you may be well aware of them already. Others of you may not have taken the time to reflect on such self-directed thoughts. So, for those of you who aren't as aware of them: think of a goal that you want to achieve. Maybe you want to find a new job. Maybe you want to earn a certain salary. Maybe you want to be married. Maybe you want to complete a certain project. Maybe you want to get a certain degree. Whatever the goal is, notice the first thought or set of thoughts that come to your mind as soon as you say that you want to achieve it. Those are the thoughts to write down.

Here are some examples of negative thoughts that you might be directing at yourself:

> - I can't do *x*.
> - I am not loved.
> - I am ugly.
> - I don't like *x* about myself.

> ➤ I will never be successful.
> ➤ They would never hire me.
> ➤ I will always be poor.
> ➤ I'm not good enough for *x*.
> ➤ I hate myself.
> ➤ I will never meet my life partner.
> ➤ I don't deserve *x*.
> ➤ I am not smart enough.

The list is endless. Now consider who else in your family you believe has the same pattern of thoughts. Write their name(s) down. It could be your mother, your father, your spouse to whom you have been married for over twenty years (energies do begin to blend), your grandparents, or others.

We can send blessings to whomever we feel may have the same pattern of negative thinking. Begin doing prayers and offerings on their behalf, to help them heal from the karmic energy of their thought pattern. In this manner we can free them as well as ourselves with blessings of peace and happiness and go more towards the root of the problem. This will loosen our own energy imprints to transform more easily, so that we can be free of the habitual negative feelings or thoughts.

Thoughts and emotions go hand in hand. Thoughts activate emotions and emotions activate thoughts. Both are energies at the core and both create the rhythm of our life.

Writing Exercise

Write down the emotions that you experience most frequently. Are they envy, jealousy, anger, helplessness, fear, revenge? Write them all down and as you look at the list, imagine how they feel in your body. If you wrote down jealousy, really feel what it feels like when you feel jealous. Where do you get tense and tight? What happens in your body in reaction to feeling that emotion?

As we mentioned before, consider who else in the family experiences those emotions frequently, and do an offering or prayer on their behalf with the intention to free them from the suffering and negative karma that those emotional patterns are bringing.

Our life, which is a reflection of our karma, has been whatever it has been in the past. To a large extent, it has been our own and our ancestors' creation. Instead of being angry at our life, our past, our mistakes, stop all thoughts for a moment and realize that we are where we are, and the story we create about our life directs the wheels of our life upon a certain path. It can continue to direct our life on the same path that we are going presently, or it can be changed. Oftentimes it's the subtler thoughts that go unnoticed that have the reigns of our life, and we wonder why our goals and desires are not manifesting and why we keep coming up against a wall. We need to address the past, not to blame or judge, but just to recognize that we are part of a lineage. We are connected to our environment. We are carrying patterns of our karma as well as our ancestors'. Though our ancestors are no longer here, our actions, thoughts, and emotions moving forward will keep impacting our karma, leading us either in the same direction or a new and different one.

The mind is constantly on, like gears turning, sending out vibrations with our thoughts and emotions. Much of the mind's movement is unnecessary and to our disadvantage; any negative thoughts towards others not only harms those people but also reverberates back to us and blocks grace in our own lives. Keeping good, positive thoughts transforms the negative ones into prayers and blessings. If your mind sees something bad, transform that into something good through prayers of blessings towards what you are seeing, or take real action to transform that bad into good.

Visualization Exercise

Sit quietly for five minutes at least once a day, closing your eyes and envisioning your mind as the sky—vast and without any cloud cover. Every morning before stepping out of your home (and ideally also before going to bed), clear the mind and imagine it as that vast blue sky. Clear your canvas of all its thoughts and perceptions and focus only on that vast blue sky. Do this daily, or better yet throughout the day, whenever you see the sky; transpose it onto your mind. Through this exercise, you will gradually train your mind to be emptier and associate it with a vast, clear stretch rather than a dense jungle.

Prayer Exercise

Spend five minutes a day praying for the well-being of all the people that you love. Think of each one specifically and send them prayers and blessings wishing them the best.

Then spend five minutes praying for the well-being of all the people who have hurt you or towards whom you have negative feelings. Even though it may be difficult, depending on how deeply they have hurt you, remember that they did so out of ignorance. In such cases, you can pray for light to fill their lives so that they can wake up from their lack of awareness. Or, if you see a specific trait in them that you know is not supportive and loving—such as jealousy, addiction, or hatred—pray for them to be free of it.

Lastly, spend five minutes praying for yourself to grow more peaceful and your mind to become more like a vast, empty blue sky—still, calm, and content. Feel what it feels like to be content, peaceful, and a vast blue sky.

Chapter 6
Heal Your Karma through Nature

"The highest education is that which does not merely give us information but makes our life in harmony with all existence."

— Rabindranath Tagore

There are many factors of existence that throw us off balance—our thoughts, our emotions, our environment, our interactions, our past traumas. They all leave imprints within our energy field, and our energy field is alive. In the same way that planting an orange seed leads to the maturation of an orange tree which bears fruit, our thoughts, emotions, and experiences plant seeds in our energy field that grow and bear their respective fruits, which can be either tasty or not so tasty.

When those fruits are positive, they make us feel happy, life flows effortlessly, and everything seems to fall into place. But when those fruits are negative, we experience tension, and whatever we want to achieve comes with a lot of difficulty. This is not to say that all of life's experiences can bring happiness or that having to put effort into something means that it's not meant to be. It means that our reactions to whatever life brings us become the cause from which future effects result.

Let's say you are going on a road trip, and as you are driving it starts to rain. You slow your speed. After a while the sky gets clear and sunny, and you drive with ease again. Then a piece of luggage falls from the top rack of the car in front of you and comes flying into your lane, making you swerve aside to avoid it. Next, as you reach an intersection, you see that the road in front of you turns into a construction zone, and now you have to take a detour to reach your destination. So you make a right and the drive takes you an hour longer, but at least you are still heading towards your destination.

This is life, throwing experiences at us. It is karma at a certain level that not only you experience but others on the road with you as well. But everyone experiencing the same roadblocks will have different reactions. Those reactions can then create either even bigger roadblocks to their destinations or open up opportunities to something they didn't expect but that could be to their benefit.

For example, let's return to the moment when it begins to rain. You have to slow down, but you are really angry that you are getting delayed. You start screaming at the cars around you for driving cautiously. In that state of frustration and fury, you don't see the bag that has gone flying off of the car in front of you. Instead of avoiding it, you notice it too late and drive right into it. You can hear your tire go flat. You slam on the brakes and the car behind you runs into your bumper. Now you have worse headaches to deal with than the rain. In this case, your anger, your reaction to the circumstance, was the cause of you losing your equilibrium and peace, hindered you from being fully alert, and set a chain reaction of events into motion in your life and your karma.

This book in your hands may have come across your path when you are twenty years old, or forty, or seventy. You have accumulated a lifetime of experiences, reactions, thoughts, and emotions that have fashioned your karma without your conscious awareness. We have reacted to many people and circumstances, we have had good or bad thoughts, and all of these have not only left an imprint in our energy field; they have created a wave that has set our life on a certain path.

Whether we are aware of it or not, we are in constant interaction with others' energy fields. When we interact with another human, we are interacting energetically with their thoughts, their emotions, their traumas, and their past. We may encounter a person while feeling happy and leave them feeling down and drained. Even if the interaction was minimal or simply work-related, for example, our energy fields interacted beyond any touch or words that were exchanged. Their sadness blended into our energy field and left an imprint that continued to impact us even after we leave them. Our bitter words leave an imprint in another's energy field long after we meet them. These imprints, whether from our own thoughts or emotions or from others or our environment, impact our perceptions, our decisions, and ultimately our karma.

Since the energy fields play such a big role in our lives and our karma, the question becomes, how do we cleanse these imprints? Not only we humans have an energy field. All of life is in fact pure energy and has an energy field—mountains, oceans, trees, animals, rocks. Everything on earth is alive and has an energy field. One of the most powerful methods for cleansing our energy field is through nature's energies. The mountains, the ocean, the sun, the earth, the wind, the trees, all have a very powerful ability to support us to be in harmony within ourselves and our environment and to cleanse the imprints that we have been carrying with us for years. Nature can help clear away the heaviness, the negative energies within our energy field. Nature's energy is like a shower that cleanses the dirt that has accumulated over the years, blocking our vision, our kindness, and our righteous decisions that lead to more grace in our lives. It is the alignment with nature that brings more harmony into our lives.

> *One of the greatest ways to transform our karma is through reverence for nature.*

When you look at nature, you see that it is always giving. The tree that gives shade to a good person will give the same relief to a thief. Swimming in the coolness of the ocean can be enjoyed by anyone, no matter who they are, what they do, or what their background is. Nature does not judge. A tree gives its fruits to anyone. The sun shines its light on anyone. This is being in a state of complete love and compassion. It is we humans that need nature. Nature does not need us. Yet nature continues to give of its abundance endlessly.

One of the greatest ways to transform our karma is through reverence for nature. With every step we take towards respecting and caring for nature, it showers its grace on our life manifold. In the ancient cultures, there was a lot of emphasis on respecting one's elders; well, in the same category with ancestors are the earth and all of nature. In the same way that we would not exist if it weren't for our ancestors, we would not be here if it were not for the earth and the sun. All of us owe our life to the earth and any harm we do to it directly impacts our karma. Our greatest teacher is nature. It teaches us about giving, compassion, and strength. Many indigenous cultures see their relationship with nature as being one of reciprocity. They understand that by protecting nature, nature in turn protects them. This mutual respect puts us in alignment to bring more grace into our lives. God is in nature, and to care for nature invites God's grace.

Remember that our thoughts are energy and that they create a reaction in our environment and in our karma. Our emotions are energy as well and, in the same manner, introduce ripples into our path of life, which is our karma. Our actions directly send waves that bring back a reaction into our life which, again, adds to our karma. Our past traumas have left imprints in our energy field that can block the flow of grace in our life and cause us to react in certain ways that create more negative karma for us. And nature is the reflection of purity, of harmony, of peace, of love, of compassion, of giving; and our relationship with it can help us cleanse our energy fields, our thoughts, our emotions, and our past traumas and bring us into alignment for peace and harmony within ourselves and our life.

How do we work with nature to bring about this change? Following are some exercises to assist you in turning your karma around through nature's power. When at all possible, do these exercises outdoors with nature surrounding you. It will help to clear the imprints left in your energy field and in your meridians and chakras. It will help open the tightness and blockage and allow for more flow so that more grace can enter your life and transform your karma.[4]

Nature Exercises

Below you will find various exercises involving nature's power. Each element of nature can be a source for cleansing. Begin and end every one of these exercises with a bow, either physically

---

[4] There are even more exercises with different elements not mentioned here, which can be found in my book *Lose Weight Unleash Your Creativity*.

or in intention. The act of bowing down is a gesture of gratitude and humility, and fostering these qualities is the first step in transforming your karma. It is actually a great daily practice: bow down before you get up from bed in the morning and bow down before going to bed in the evening. In this act of bowing down to nature, you are cleansing yourself before your day begins and as your day ends, emptying yourself of all negativity and washing it away from your head down into the earth. Thank Mother Nature and thank all those who have crossed your path during the day. Thank your family and give thanks for your life. Set your intention to have your heart be filled with compassion and respect every day.

The Sun

Light is a powerful agent to remove blockages that we have accumulated over our lifetime as a result of our thoughts, emotions, and actions. The greatest source of light is the sun. Whether the sun is shining or hiding behind the clouds, imagine allowing its rays to fill your body. You can do this at any time of the day, but it is best to start your day with it. Before getting out of bed, imagine the rays of the sun entering through the top of your head all the way down to your feet and filling you with golden light. Feel the rays penetrating all parts of your body, the front, the back, the top, the bottom. Feel it energizing your body and washing away all the blockages, all the negative thoughts, all the painful emotions, all the painful memories, any anxiety, worry, anger, fear.

Then focus on the center of your chest and envision the sun's rays penetrating the heart center, filling it with golden light. Feel the peace and the sun's grace moving through your heart and expanding throughout the rest of your body. See it overflowing beyond your body into the energy field surrounding you and filling it with golden light as well.

This exercise can also be used for particular situations of conflict with another person. Instead of reacting negatively, which will only bring about more negative reaction from the other, send the sun's energy to surround the person involved in the conflict. It may or may not change the circumstance, but it can change your response to it, which will most definitely improve your future karma.

The Sky

In the same way that the sky expands into infinity, so does it bring that vast awareness to us when we allow ourselves to merge with it in our meditation. This is a good exercise to perform before going to bed or during times when you feel stuck in a circumstance, unable to discern your options. Throughout the day, we may experience different situations that cause us to tense up and form blockages in our energy. These blockages don't always simply go away. If we were to step into a puddle of muddy water, simply stepping out from it would not get the mud off us. We would have to consciously clean our shoes. So it is with the interactions in our life—they often leave residues in our energy field that can only be cleared if we use our intention to do so.

As you lay in bed, feel your body being filled with the light blue of the sky. Even though it may be nighttime, imagine the sky as being filled with light and your body as expanding with it into the infinite. Breathe deeply and feel yourself expanding. See yourself as being larger and more expansive than the person that you know to be. Let your thoughts become still, peaceful, and vast like

115

the sky. Let your heart open and feel the sky and the universe beyond within you.

The Earth

The earth is the greatest resource for transforming our energy. In the same manner that it takes food waste and transforms it into compost, it can absorb our negative energy, thoughts, and emotions and transform them. When you feel the energy of anger or anxiety in your daily life, whether towards yourself or another person or situation, take a deep breath and let the negative energy fall through your feet into the earth. And in return, let the earth's power rise through your feet and fill your body with its strength and peace. Do this several times: release your negative energy into the earth and allow the earth's power to fill you back up.

The earth sustains us while we are alive, and we return back to the earth when we die. It is pure compassion, holding us in its lap from the beginning of our life until the end. Simply remembering this fact can bring us into a state of compassion and humility.

The Waterfall

Water has a great power to purify and refresh the energy field. Imagine yourself standing under a gentle, slightly cool waterfall in a beautiful nature scene. Feel the water showering over your body softly and clearing away painful memories, negative thoughts in your mind, hurt emotions, and all that might be stemming from your ancestors.

These are just a few practices to help transform your energy with the support of nature's power. Many of us feel very disconnected from nature, especially living a city life. And in our everyday busyness we create blockages that form the direction of our life. We hardly take the time to reflect on our past and how we are carrying it with us, dormant in our energy field. These blockages and dormant traumas are like a rudder in a boat: though they are not visible above the water's surface, they are changing our course.

Even if you forget to connect with nature, one thing that you do not forget is to breathe, and you can use your breath for healing. While maintaining consciousness of your breath for a few minutes every day, use your intention to breathe out the pain, the sadness, the anxiety, the negative thoughts, the anger, the frustration; and breathe in peace, happiness, equanimity, love, forgiveness, and nature's power. You can do this anywhere—at school, on your lunch break at work, while sitting on your couch, or traveling by airplane. Remember that daily interactions, thoughts, and emotions are like dust particles left in the energy field. They become the invisible wind that changes our direction in life for better or worse. Therefore, at the very least using our intention to neutralize the negative energies with positive ones is a good starting point.

Your home is an extension of you. In the same way that walking into your house with your shoes on brings in the dirt from outside, so are your experiences throughout the day carried with you into your home through your energy field. These energies accumulate over time. Opening the windows for the wind to move though our home and clear the stagnant energy which has accumulated is a good daily habit to foster.

Plants are very powerful and have very unique energetic properties. Drinking certain herbal teas can have a medicinal impact on our health, and similarly, burning certain plants in the form of incense can have a purifying impact on our energy field and home. Frankincense, rue, and sage are powerful plants for clearing stagnation and negativity in the environment.

Cleansing is a very important aspect of resetting the physical body and the energy field. Essentially, what the awareness and cleansing process does is remind us of the bigger picture: who we are and our interconnection with all of life. As a result, we come to recognize our immense responsibility towards all of creation, with the knowledge that harming another will harm us. The pain of another will become our pain. The harmful reactions we have will return to us and harm us. Putting a dagger into the energy of another through our reactions or thoughts will be simultaneously putting one in our own. We just may not realize it at the time. Nature is our ally to bring us back to love, compassion, and humility so that the waves of our karma take us in the direction of greater happiness.

Chapter 7
Giving—The Secret of Karma

"True happiness is when the love that is within us finds expression in external activities."

— Mata Amritanandamayi

When people speak about wanting to change their karma, what they often mean is they want more positive experiences in their life. Instead of constant roadblocks, they are looking for more harmony, peace, and ease. Karma is the law of reaction to an action that took place recently, a long time ago, or even in another lifetime (for those who believe in reincarnation) and is returning to us in the present. The present is the fruit of our past. The future will be the fruit of our present and past. Therefore, to change the future, we need to transform the past and make wise choices in the present.

To turn the momentum of the past around more positively, the greatest thing that we can do is give. The secret to grace is in giving; that is, giving opens the heart to receive grace. When we are in a state of constant taking or of negative thoughts and emotions, we have no space inside for grace. Grace is like a gentle breeze flowing toward us. If we have surrounded ourselves with walls of hate, anger, or selfishness, a gentle breeze can't penetrate into our heart. It takes a tornado to shake us. And that is exactly what often happens: tornados of unexpected circumstances crash into our life. An accident, a loss of a job or a relationship, a burglary of our car or home, or a myriad of other adverse situations. These situations come basically to break our wall, to give us the opportunity to grow more humble, kinder, more giving, so that grace can enter and fill our life with blessings. When our ego takes up the space within us, it leaves no room for anything else but a battle. When we rid ourselves of the ego, then we allow space for grace and its blessings. It's only when one sees oneself as part of the world—of animals, of plants, of other people—that the ego can step aside. By seeing oneself connected to God's creation, the channels open up in one's life for the power of this creation to pour in. As long as we feel separated from all that is around us, our hearts will remain closed. Grace can only fully flow into an open heart. The greater the openness of the heart, the greater its capacity for grace to flow in.

Giving requires a certain mindset. It is always asking, "What can I do for others?" and "What is needed in this situation that I can assist with?" Unfortunately, though, most of us often find ourselves asking, "What can I get from this situation or person?" We calculate our interactions, our circle of acquaintances, and our decisions in general, by the metric of how they will serve us. We think about what we can get from a partner or from our job. We like to accumulate things, judging more as better. One car becomes two, two becomes three. We need a second phone, a second girlfriend or boyfriend, another walk-in closet for our fifty pairs of shoes, and a new home with greater square footage. There is nothing wrong with having things. We just need to see the balance in our life between taking and holding on and giving. If we take the time to sincerely reflect on our life, how much are we truly giving? How much are we helping others? How much do we support people in need, whether with our time or financially? How much are we truly thinking about the less fortunate? How much are we showing love to our family? How much time are we giving our family?

We can have a lot and be a taker, or we can have very little and be a taker. It's really not about money or material possessions. It's about love. It's about having our eyes open for chances to offer help. It's about seeing an elderly person needing help with their grocery bags and going up to them. It's about recognizing that someone else is weaker in a certain skill and going to their aid humbly. It's about noticing how hot it is outside and leaving water for the animals and birds. It's about consciously not buying a plastic water bottle when you have a choice, so that you cause less stress to the environment. It's about having a mind-set of abundance, a cup that is overflowing with love. There are many who are very wealthy but have a mind-set of a beggar—a mind-set that says one has nothing to give. A beggarly mind-set feels lack, even if the person has a lot. A truly rich mind-set is one of abundance; such a person may own very little but will happily give of that little if another needs it.

I remember while traveling within Bolivia in South America. I was on a twelve-hour bus ride, coming back from the mountains after a trekking journey. It was a very old bus, very loud and completely packed. Next to me was an elderly Bolivian lady. She very clearly had very little money. She took out some food from her small bag, turned to me, and offered some to me. I will always remember her kindness. This wasn't the only time I've experienced overwhelming generosity from someone of very little means. I have traveled quite a lot to many parts of the world that are considerably poor and have always come across such giving hearts.

On another trip to Mumbai, India, many years ago, I stopped to ask a lady for directions. She was with her daughter and instead of just telling me where to go, she invited me to her home. She prepared lunch for me, we talked for some time, and then she went with me to the place I was looking for. Her home was only a very small room, yet her heart was abundant. She helped me constantly until we parted ways.

Sometimes we tell ourselves, "When I have certain amount of money, then I can support some charity or I will contribute to such-and-such a cause." But what's important to be aware of is that giving has no price tag or income bracket. It does not require the "right" time or place or circumstances, or even the "right" amount. Giving is a state of mind that can follow us every day in everything that we do. It's a heart that is filled with compassion. It's a heart that prays for others, that gives to others, that looks to fill what is missing for others. Things don't have to be going perfectly in one's life in order to give. By giving, everything in one's life starts to become more perfect.

When we open our heart's eyes, we see the world very differently than through our physical eyes. We truly see people. We don't just pass by them. We see what they need. Do they need kindness? Give them a smile and a few minutes of your time. Are they having a bad day? If you are near a coffee shop, buy them a coffee, just because. Are they stressed? Pray for them in your mind and send them happiness, or if they are a friend, take them somewhere to make them happy. Are they struggling financially? Buy them something they need, give them a little bit of your abundance, or give them a discount on something. Are they looking weak? Buy them lunch, take them to have their health checked, or buy them some vitamins. Are they feeling lonely? Take a couple of hours a week to spend with them or call them every day to speak for a few minutes. Are they feeling lost in their life? Buy them a book that might inspire them, give them some advice, or offer them a job. Are they feeling disempowered? Give them a compliment. Do something unexpected to make another happy. Even if it's not a special occasion, perform a small gesture of thoughtfulness for another. Write a review for a business you appreciate. Send a thank-you card to someone just for being who they are. It doesn't always take a lot to make a difference. Make a point of doing just *one* thing, however small, to make another happy. The least expensive and least time-consuming of all is a genuine smile.

> *Make it a daily habit to give something, however big or small, from your heart to another.*

Giving isn't about money, though that can certainly be one aspect of it. We can give clothes, hugs, a hand to hold, an ear to listen, a smile, a peaceful presence, a bag of groceries, or a helping hand; we can leave seeds for the birds or refrain from killing a spider in favor of taking it outside; and so much more. Giving is about an act that makes another happy and reduces their suffering. It's an act that shows that you care about someone close to you, a complete stranger, an animal, nature, or the planet. In caring, one gives. In giving, one receives grace, which in turn transforms one's karma.

How do you find people or causes that you can give to?

Do your research and find an organization that you know dedicates 100% (or close to 100%)

of their donations to help the poor or another important cause. Offer your time there or donate to them. Even if it's a small amount of time or money, take the step. Find organizations that help children, the elderly, the poor, nature, or animals, and support them. Do your research to be sure that the organization is truly doing what they say they are doing and that their donations are truly supporting that cause.

Even helping a single child is a tremendous act of giving. In many countries, children need only $1 per day to be able to go to school. In some countries, elderly need only $80 per month to be able to live. Think of that! Even $1 given is better than none. The smallest act of giving brings with it so much grace, and the biggest part of that grace is the happiness one feels within from simply making another happy. That happiness itself shifts the mind to be more positive and to turn one's karma around.

There are many children, apart from one's own, that need help. Many of them are in orphanages. Many are so poor they hardly have any clothing or food. Many cannot afford to buy the supplies for school or even pay for school at all.

Some are raised in homes where they don't receive love. We may not be able to help all children everywhere, but if each of us were to take just one child anywhere in the world under our wing and care for them as our little sister or brother, imagine how many children would get support.

The elderly are often neglected at the most difficult stage in their lives. They are often extremely alone with no one to talk to. They lack warmth and the simple human touch, a hug, a hand on their shoulder, a smile. In many poor countries, the elderly have to beg for food. Imagine being at the vulnerable age of ninety years old and needing to beg for survival. Most of us will be old one day and in need of care in some form or another. We will not remain strong and capable of being independent forever. We will not always have all the friends we have around us now. If you know of anyone who is in their golden years or even someone whom you don't know but is in a home, take the time to visit with them. Listen to them. Let them pour out their heart, even if what they are saying may not make sense all the time. Oftentimes they are incapable of driving around to places on their own; so put aside a few hours a month to take someone for a drive to their favorite restaurant or a scenic place, or just simply for a drive, so they can see something other than the four walls they eat and sleep within. Look at the world through their eyes. Put yourself in their shoes, Make a difference in someone else's life.

I was sitting outdoors in a restaurant once when a homeless man walked by. He stopped and complimented me on my sweater. When I thanked him and told him my mother had knitted it, his eyes filled with tears. He told me that his mother had died when he was really young. When we see homeless people, we might have a tendency to walk faster, look away, or cross the street. But it's important to know that they all have a story that brought them to where they are. Being homeless is not a stamp that has been branded on their forehead. Circumstances in their past were such that they were not able to handle the pain or the stress. They fell and were never able to pick themselves up again. Sometimes it takes only an understanding heart for them to be seen for the first time, to be heard for the first time, to be treated with respect as a human for the first time. If you see a homeless person, give them something to eat. It might be just a banana, but it acknowledges that they exist. Sometimes take the time to listen to their life stories. Give them a smile. Say hello. Send your blessings to them. When I have helped a friend, the most I have usually received back was a thank you. But when I have helped the homeless, the majority of them say "God bless you," some have even kissed my hand. Imagine, they are the ones without a roof over their head, and they are sending me their blessings. Their hearts are still generous enough to do so. Through all of their poverty, challenges, and struggles, they have maintained their gratitude for the small things.

Apart from our pets, we often neglect animals and take their lives for granted. But every creature has its own sufferings. Every creature longs to live. In our ignorance, we assume that they don't have feelings and harming them or killing them is nothing significant. Whether it's a small spider, a fly, an elephant, a bird, or a fish, all animals long to live. Not a single one enjoys suffering or wants to die. In the same way that we would run away from a gunshot, if we could, they too would run from their death. In the same way that we have a family—a mother, a father, and siblings—so do they. Many animal farms hurt animals by abusing them, making them live in unbearable situations with no room to move. At times they are starved or they are fed food that is unhealthy. They are injected with hormones to grow at a faster rate for more profit. There are organizations that rescue such abused animals when they can and care for them. We can give to such organizations by supporting them financially or volunteering to help care for the animals. I have done both and I can only say how extremely fulfilling it is. I am not sure who is helping who— me the animals or the animals me. They are so loving and pure to be around that I always feel happier after leaving. These organizations often offer the chance for people to adopt an animal and support it financially. Of course, we can also adopt pets and care for them in our homes, but this should only be done if we can truly care for them. We can also make a decision to reduce support for all the animal slaughtering that happens by reducing our meat intake—whether it's chicken, beef, turkey, fish, pork, or any other animal flesh. We can make a conscious decision to eat meat only one or two times per week or completely stop, if possible. Not only can fasting from meat be very good for the body; but by doing so, we reduce the suffering that animals undergo by being killed. Make a point of putting food out for the birds and squirrels. Educate yourself on what they actually eat, rather than just leaving bread and other human foods for them.

Volunteering is a wonderful way to give, especially if it's done from the heart. Objects or money come and go throughout one's lifetime. But time is one thing that is limited. A day that is gone will be gone forever. Thus, volunteering is giving of the most precious thing one has. One could be doing many things, but a volunteer chooses to donate their limited time to help another. There are so many that require support, from children, to the elderly, to animals, to nature. Spending one's time volunteering with children to educate them, to support them emotionally, to take them on a trip to experience something new, to care for them, to listen to them, are just some of the ways in which we could give. Taking time to listen to the elderly, helping them take care of themselves when they are not able to, taking them somewhere that makes them happy, are all donations of our time. Feeding the animals in an animal rescue facility, caring for their health, cleaning their living area, planting trees, planting a garden for the homeless, are examples of time well spent.

Our state of mind is an act of giving, if we direct it in the right way. We are given so much in life that we often overlook and take for granted. The simple act of gratitude is an act of giving back. Lack of gratitude can block positive things from coming into our lives. A lot of times people wonder why they feel stuck; why, no matter how hard they try, they are not able to manifest the things they are longing for. The lack of gratitude is one of the biggest roadblocks. If we aren't happy with whatever we have, however little it is, how can we have space for more? Gratitude opens the door to grace and increases our receptivity to it. The heart opens when we feel gratitude. But often, when we are confronted with circumstances that displease or distress us, we forget the good things that we have despite those circumstances. And in that moment, we close the door of receptivity. It is a good exercise in those moments, when circumstances are adverse, to be grateful for one thing that makes you happy. Anything. It may be completely unrelated to the situation, but just remember to be grateful for it in the midst of your discomfort and disappointment. A good way to make this a habit is to write down one thing that you are grateful for every single day.

Sometimes it requires comparisons to appreciate what one has. Driving an old car may seem like a burden when you have to always be worried about it breaking down. But when you see people who can't afford a car and have to instead either walk or take a bus for hours to get to where they need to, it can make you more grateful for the old car you have. When you are really hungry and get upset because all you can find nearby is a salad bar when you really want Thai food, think of someone in another part of the world who is lucky if they have even a piece of bread to eat today. It's important to travel in order to open one's eyes and heart; seeing how others live gives us more awareness of how grateful we should be for what we have. Compassion increases when we see others and their lives and struggles.

From the time we are born, we breathe, we bathe with water, we enjoy the sunshine, we sit and play under tree canopies, and we eat fruits and vegetables and grains. As much as we may use and enjoy nature, we don't realize the unfathomable power that it has—and its utter selflessness. Our existence is completely dependent on nature. Without the earth that allows us to make our home on it, the sun that gives its warmth to us and allows plants and food to grow, the waters that quench our thirst, help us to be clean, and support plants to grow, and the plants themselves that grow and become food for us, we would not be able to live. The trees are our source of oxygen. The plants are our source of nourishment. We take continuously from nature, yet rarely do we think about giving back. Nature is our first mother and father, without which our human parents would not be alive. Hence, it requires our utmost respect and reverence. Yet we often treat it with entitlement and neglect. When we protect and care for nature, it showers its grace and protection upon us manifold.

In the olden days, in many parts of the world, people began their day giving offerings to Mother Nature, bowing down to it, and always remembering that their life depended on it. We can make it a habit every morning and evening, after waking up and before going to bed, to bow down our heads to nature and give our thanks. We can give offerings to the earth of just a little bit of water or seeds. It's the gesture that opens the heart and opens the door for grace to come into our lives. We can consume fewer animal products when possible so that we can support the life of animals.

As we spoke about earlier, our thoughts are energy and are a form of "giving." If we put out negative thoughts, we are giving that to our surroundings. And the seeds of our thoughts come from our perception. Our perception forms the types of thoughts that we have, and those thoughts become the precursor of our actions. If we see life as sacred, we take care of it more. If we see our family, our coworkers, and nature as sacred, we give them a greater level of care. This care returns back to us as grace. If we feel isolated, we see our actions as having no repercussions. Yet the fact remains that we are interdependent on other human beings, all animals, and all of nature. We can only see and feel this if our heart is open. And an open heart is a vessel to receive grace.

Giving is truly the greatest way to transform one's karma.

Chapter 8
Plant Your Visions

"Reach high, for stars lie hidden in you.
Dream deep, for every dream precedes the goal."
— Rabindranath Tagore

K arma is the fruit of the seeds we have planted and the weeds that may have grown around them. In following the suggestions in the previous chapters, we have prepared the soil and pulled the weeds of our negative karma. It is at this point that we are ready for planting the new seeds for our healthy visions of our future. Many times in life, we want certain things and we wonder why they don't manifest. Yet with the poor soil conditions of our mind and our actions, we ourselves have blocked the manifestation of our dreams. Once the soil is prepared, there is space and fertile ground for the sunlight to help our visions to grow.

Writing Exercise

To start this process of planting new seeds, take your notebook and write your list of dreams and visions for your life, from the very small ones to big ones. There is something about writing the words that instills extra power in them and gives a more targeted direction for the energies of your life. You can write not only the final goal but also the steps you need to take to reach that goal, as goals in and of themselves.

For example, let's say you are struggling with a health condition. You can write: *Be free from my chronic headaches.* But underneath, also write: *Research doctors to find a cure for my headaches. Manifest the resources for learning about the root cause of my headaches. Find a natural cure or relief for my headaches. Have the strength to find a solution to overcome my headaches. Start eating healthier. Start drinking more water. Stop drinking soda pop. Stop eating sugar.*

You see how there are layers to the vision? The steps toward the final vision are just as important as the final vision itself. Sometimes aiming for the goal directly, which may be aiming very high, can be discouraging if we don't reach it as soon as we would like to. Therefore, writing down more steps that lead to the vision is also important, even though sometimes visions are manifested suddenly in unexpected ways. You may find yourself reaching your goal by skipping over the steps prior. Or you may find that you achieve it gradually, one step at a time.

Let's take another example: you would like to earn more money. You could write on your list of visions simply that you want to make more money, or write a specific amount that you would like to make per month or year.

And underneath, write: *Find companies that I would enjoy working for and would pay me* x amount. *Re-do my resume. Send out two resumes per week. Brainstorm new ways to support myself in making* x amount. *Get inspired to learn what my passion is and earn* x amount *by pursuing it. Find ways to earn* x amount *in a way that makes me happy. Find a position at the following companies and earn* x amount. There are many ways to write your vision.

As I mentioned before, nature has tremendous power to support us. Writing your visions down at the start of a new moon when the moon is building its energy in the waxing phase towards being full, or just a few days before it is full, gives more power to your visions. We are connected with all of nature, and nature can support us in manifesting our highest potential and our dreams. If we are looking to let go of the past, the best time to perform rituals are when the moon is going from a full moon to a new moon (the waning phase), as it is decreasing in size and power. However, the best time to manifest and start new beginnings is when the moon is a new moon going towards full, or shortly before it is full.

There are several other beneficial times of day and of the year to prepare our visions. One is our birthdays, when all of the energies are concentrated on us and astrologically the sun is in our birth sign. This gives extra fuel for manifesting, like adding fertilizer to the seedbed. On New Year's Eve, there is generally a worldwide energy of celebration. Energies are focused and we can use that to support our visions and dreams. Eclipses are another powerful time for manifesting. The hours leading to the peak of the eclipse are very powerful for prayer and help in manifesting your dreams. Before sunrise is yet another powerful time to write your visions. The sun and the moon play an influential role in the cycles of life and creation.

Nature in general is an immense support for preparation of visions. Simply sitting under a tree, on top of a mountain, by a waterfall, or near the ocean can support you in manifesting your visions as you write them down. Nature is the ultimate creator, manifesting magic in all instances. Just see how a tiny seed sprouts into a majestic tree. See how the waters of the ocean come as waves and recede to be taken up into the sky, to come back as rain onto the earth, and to join the ocean once again through the rivers. We take it for granted, yet nature can leave us speechless with its power. All of nature is alive and offers tremendous support if we work with its energy and respect it. Ask the mountains or the earth to help support your vision and give you strength and grounding to reach your goals. Ask the sky to help expand your mind to possibilities you've never dreamed of in making your dream a reality; and allow the sky's grace to fill you and inspire you in seeing ways to fashion that new reality.

Just as not every seed will open and sprout, so too with dreams. We can't force an outcome. We make it clear by writing it down and doing our best to prepare the soil and nourish the seed, and then we must surrender. Of course, we can examine what may be lacking in order for it to grow. Have we put in the necessary effort? Have we prepared the ground enough through offerings to heal our past karmic creations? Do we have any beliefs within us that could be creating obstacles to its growth? Sometimes we think we have cleared the ground, but the roots of certain karmas go so deep that they need a lot more transformation to be dug up. And certain karmas are simply destiny. But a great amount of karma can be changed if we put in the right effort.

When we make our list of visions without having cleared enough of the internal or external obstacles, our vision either doesn't manifest until we have done so, or it sets changes in motion in your life that must take place before it can manifest. Those are dreams that don't follow a straight line to manifest. They travel through unexpected pathways until they reach their destination. For example, we may accept a job at a certain company that isn't exactly where we want to work, in order to learn certain skills that will take us to the next level. Or we may need to meet someone at that company that will move to another company and take us with them. We may want to be in a relationship, and it isn't until we have experienced certain people that we come to truly appreciate the person we ultimately meet and marry.

Our visions can be for ourselves or for our family. Family is an extension of ourselves, after all. It's important not to impose our vision on our family, unless it's a general vision of well-being. It's very important, however, to have a vision of peace, success, and good health for our family. Their success only adds to our happiness. Their good health adds to our peace of mind. Their happiness adds to our happiness. For example, a mother can have the vision to be healthy and hold the same vision for her family as well. They may or may not go along with that vision, but she can maintain her vision nevertheless. Her vision plants a seed of positive creation for her family members, though it may never manifest, or it may manifest over time. As she holds the vision for herself and allows it to manifest in her own life, with time, simply by example, she may impact those around her. Like a flower that blossoms and shows its beauty for all to see, a person can inspire those close to them.

Writing Exercise

What are the kinds of things you can create visions for? Take out your notebook and start thinking about what you wish for in the following areas of your life.

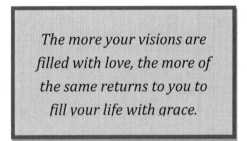

The more your visions are filled with love, the more of the same returns to you to fill your life with grace.

Home

Your home is where you spend a great majority of your time. Envision where you would like to live, the city or the country that would make you happy. Imagine the type of home that you wish for and the environment that it's set in. Is it in a city or the countryside? What kinds of views do you have from the home? Are there a lot of windows or is it dark inside? Is it one story? Is it multi story? How many rooms? Write down the things that truly matter to you.

Health

Your health is what maintains you throughout your life. If you are struggling with health issues, there is always something you can do to support improving your health—through your diet or lifestyle choices, finding the right doctor, reducing stress, creating harmony in your home, and so on. Of course, your vision is to be healthy and vital, but write more specifically what you want healed in your body. And write the steps that you find can take you there. How do you wish your body to look? How much do you want to weigh? What health issue do you want to be free of? Maybe you need to read more books to see all your options for healing. Maybe you need to get a second or third opinion about those options. Maybe you need to look at alternative ways of healing. Maybe there are supplements that would help you. Maybe you need to change your diet. List the steps that you can take to make your vision a reality to the greatest extent possible.

Career

Your work is what sustains many aspects of your life and takes a lot of your time. Though many people work a job which they don't fully enjoy or which does not pay what they wish to earn, it's important to have your work be something that not only supports you financially, but also makes you happy. Most people spend at least thirty to forty hours a week at their job. That's a lot of hours dedicated towards something one is not happy with. Envision how many hours you would like to work. What is the distance you would like to commute to work? What kind of a boss do you want to have? What kind of work would you like to do? What position would you like to have? How much money do you want to earn per hour, month, or year? What kind of responsibilities do you want to have? How much vacation time would you like? Write all this down.

Many equate work with money alone. Financial security is important. However, sometimes money itself will create a cycle of negative karma that will come to haunt us down the line. Money is a form of energy that seems to alter many people's personalities when they attain or lose it. It touches on the deepest sense of survival that can ignite a lot of fear, a lot of greed, and a lot of ego. With that false sense of power, one can lose one's conscience and travel down a selfish road that sets our positive karma on a downward spiral. It's important when envisioning greater abundance for yourself to practice humility and generosity.

Relationship

Do you want to be in a relationship? What are the qualities you are looking for in the other? What moral values do they have? What is their appearance like? How many children do they want? What kind of lifestyle do they lead? Do they like to travel? Are they affectionate? Are they more introverted or extroverted? Have they done some inner work, or does it not matter to you? What kind of job do they have? Is it important for you that they work? If you are already in a relationship, envision the qualities that sustain you both and the atmosphere you wish to create. Relationship is one of the areas where your vision can feel like it's just not sprouting. A great part of this vision manifesting is your own inner work and clearing karma on a deep level. Sometimes it's not only your own karma, but that of your ancestors that you carry when it comes to relationships. If this is an area where you feel your vision is stuck, go back to performing rituals of healing the past by doing offerings for anyone whom you may have inadvertently hurt or who has hurt you.

The people that surround us play a big role in our well-being. Write down the qualities of the types of people that you want in your life. Whether it's an intimate relationship, your family, or your coworkers. Our relationships, however close or distant, impact us.

Relationships are ultimately about sharing love. Holding onto anger, resentment, and hurt inflicted on us in the past or that we have inflicted on others can hold back the manifestation of love in our life. By becoming clear about our vision of the types of relationships and interactions we want, we set the wheels in motion for removing the obstacles so that we can make that vision a reality in our life.

Inner Self

Our inner self development sets the tone of our life. Who do we want to be? Are we being our best self? We all appreciate people who are kind, compassionate, patient, happy, peaceful, helpful, generous, wise, and intelligent. Yet we often fall short of those qualities within ourselves. It takes courage to look at ourselves honestly and see our anger, our tendency to gossip about others, our hate, our arrogance, our lack of compassion, our fear, our sadness, our constant procrastination, or our laziness. What is your vision for the ideal you? Will it make you a better person? We want to be the kind of person who creates positive karma in our life, a person whose actions and thoughts return more harmony and love into our life in the cycle of karma. See yourself as you wish to be. Write down the qualities that you want to develop and nurture in yourself.

Our visions can be about anything. They can be narrow visions that focus on our immediate needs and desires, such as a relationship, work, or financial status; or, they can be vast, with focuses such as the planet or our personal spiritual

151

evolution. What is it that you want to create? After you have written down your visions, lie down and visualize what you have written as if it's a movie in front of you. See yourself in the relationship you want. See yourself in the position you want, in the home that you want, exuding the qualities that you want. See yourself free of your health issue. See your vision as a reality in your mind's eye. Feel that vision as a reality within your body. And then surrender yourself to the vision to manifest in its time. Feeling and seeing your vision prepares your body energetically for a new vibration and helps remove the obstacles that could be in its way. The more your visions are filled with love, the more of the same returns to you to fill your life with grace. Place your list of visions in an area of your home close to a window for the sunlight to shine on it, and then surrender.

Conclusion

"Every leaf that grows will tell you:
What you sow will bear fruit.
So if you have any sense my friend,
Don't plant anything but Love."
— Rumi

The accumulation of karma throughout our and our ancestors' lifetimes determines the direction of our future. Whether that future is a pleasant or unpleasant one depends largely on the quality of the seeds planted. As much as we do to clear away the weeds and bad seeds which have taken root, it also matters which new seeds we are planting every day. In other words, it's important to develop rituals for cleansing ourselves to keep us on track to continuously improve our karma.

As explained before, karma is ultimately energy we have sent out at some point in time being sent back to us. These energies originate in the forms of actions, words, emotions, and thoughts. They can also be inherited from our ancestors. We may inadvertently send out harmful energies towards others that return into our lives to create a change in the course of our karma which is different than what we wish for. It's for this reason that we have to continuously purify ourselves and keep the channels open. Otherwise, what we have manifested can again be taken away. We need to nurture the results of our good karma for them to keep flourishing. This nurturing and purifying should take place on many levels, and in this chapter we will discuss the practices that can support you in doing so from different angles and review all that we have discussed thus far.

Your home is your place of refuge. It is the external physical structure that holds your space. It is the energy that you come home to every day and spend your nights in. It is where you keep all your belongings. It is also the place that holds the space for you while you are away at work, at school, or traveling. Once a month, put a day aside to de-clutter your home. Look through every room, closet, and cabinet and see what you have accumulated that either you don't need or that you don't love and put it aside. If there are things that still haven't found their place, re-arrange things until it feels right. Get rid of anything that you don't need, that you don't love, or that just doesn't feel good to you.

If there is any item that was given to you that you don't even like but are keeping just because, let it go. Your house should be a place that holds all that is either necessary or dear to you, not a storage shelter. Every item collects energy; a gift contains the energy of the giver. The energies which a gifted item gathers can impact your life. The giver's life circumstance, their emotional state, their intention in giving to you will all be carried within their gift to you.

Your body is your temple that carries you throughout your life. If you don't take care of it, it will fail on you or become weak, and this will impact your mind and consequently your actions, thoughts, and emotions. Therefore, taking care of your body is critical for your overall well-being as well as the repercussions it can have on your karma.

Once a week, take one day where you eat only vegetables and fruits and drink a lot of water as well as juices and herbal teas. Give your body time to rest and let the toxins clear out of your body. Avoid meats, processed foods, dairy, nuts, and bread on this day. Eat as light as possible. Give your mind time to rest and let it be a day that you replenish yourself.

Our body accumulates toxins over a lifetime of eating the wrong foods and being exposed to pesticides and pollution, which can impact our mind and emotions over time. But it also accumulates toxins energetically from all of our daily interactions. Exercises with nature, such as the ones I have described in this book, can be done regularly to wash away all the heaviness in your mind and emotions which sprung from all the harsh interactions you experienced.

Each evening before bed, take the time to reflect on your day, starting from the moment that you woke up. Review all the interactions that you had, however wonderful, stressful, painful, frustrating, or sad they were. Were you hurt by anyone? Did you hurt anyone? Did you hurt nature in any way? Every day is an opportunity to learn to forgive, to purify, and to create new paths for your future karma. Holding onto resentment, anger, and pain will only plant those seeds for your future karma to attract. Having hurt another person or part of nature also will set into motion repercussions in the future. This review of your day gives you the opportunity to do ritual offerings in which you either forgive or ask for forgiveness. If someone did something good for you, if you received food from nature, if you received a gift, this is your opportunity to send blessings to the source of that good. Gratitude is the greatest way to turn your life around. Life is about reciprocity, give-and-take. When we receive blessings from others, it's important to return those blessings to them. In this manner, we lubricate the wheel of positive karma in our life.

It can be challenging to be honest with ourselves about how our actions could be harming another. Whether at the end of each day or once a week, we need to look at ourselves honestly and see what old habits we are repeating that are hard to break. If we don't reflect on them, there is a tendency to perform them over and over, digging their negative karma deeper into our life. We need to see where we are being selfish at the expense of others; where we are taking from others without giving back; where we are playing with people's hearts to serve our own needs; where we are simply using someone without thinking about their well-being. Where is greed creeping into our life? Where are we carrying anger or negative feelings about someone? Any action that ultimately harms someone else will set the stage for harm coming back to us in some form or another. If we steal from someone, it may not happen that that same person steals from us or even that some other person steals from us, but something else that is dear to us may be taken away—whether it's our health, a family member's health, or our job. Karma comes back, but sometimes through a side door. That's why some people cannot recognize the result of their actions directly.

Some things are harder to let go of; even after doing many offerings and prayers, the pain or anger remains. These feelings can be so deep rooted that they require a constant chiseling away to be transformed. It is a helpful practice to spend time once a month doing an offering of sweets, flower, or incense for those that we hold anger towards or those whom we have hurt. We can never pray enough for the good of others. With every prayer to forgive, we ourselves become free. Even if all things in our life are good, we can do offerings for unknowingly having harmed another or unknowingly harboring negative thoughts towards others. Simply giving gratitude for those who are in our life and who support us, the food that we eat, and the home that we live in, is itself an offering. Nothing should be taken for granted. There is always a lot to be grateful for.

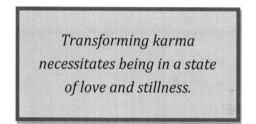

Transforming karma necessitates being in a state of love and stillness.

Our actions are often a result of our state of mind and emotions. Our mind is often like the wind, shifting erratically without any control. The smallest unpleasant gesture from someone can make our mind react. Being stuck in traffic can make our mind react; someone bumping into us at the market can make us react. And all of our reactions lead to repercussions within the law of karma. Living in a very active world, it seems difficult to find hours in the day to eat or sleep enough, let alone meditate. However, meditation can support all of the activities of the day to run more smoothly and harmoniously, softening the edges of our usual reactions. Meditation doesn't have to be a long, drawn-out process that requires rigid positions and hours of sitting still. It can be five minutes of sitting silently, quieting the mind, watching our breath, and listening to the sound of the wind or the ocean (whether it's the actual wind or ocean or a recording). It's important to take a little bit of time out of a busy day and simply stop and do nothing. If watching your breath or your thoughts come and go is difficult, then listen to a guided visualization as a form of meditation that allows your body and mind to relax and become quiet.

With practice, we can take better control of the reigns of our thoughts and emotions and prevent them from creating unnecessary bad karma for us. Like a young child in a store who may run away and break items on the shelves, our mind, if not under our control, can get away from us and create repercussions that we may not suspect are related to the unpleasant circumstances of our life.

Five or ten minutes should be the minimum daily time we give to solitude in order to bring harmony to our mind and life. These days we are all running from point A to point B, texting and talking on the phone, watching television, preparing dinner, shopping for things we need. There is noise constantly all around us. There is so much noise, in fact, that we need to tune out the majority of it to maintain our sanity. But even if we tune it out, that doesn't mean that it does not impact our energy field and the waves of our mind anyway. Have you ever gone from a very noisy restaurant to the streets in a small town where there is complete silence in the evening? Have you noticed the rapid difference and how your body suddenly relaxes in the silence? Now expand that silence to an entire day. Imagine if you were to spend an entire day without the phone, without any television, without any radio or music but simply in silence. Imagine that all that you could hear was the sound of the wind in the trees, the birds, and the distant sound of a dog's bark. Nothing else. How would you feel?

For most, it would be quite a challenge. But such silence is cleansing and rejuvenating for the energy body and mind, like fasting is to the physical body. Spend a day in nature under some trees, by a river, or on a mountain. Sit in solitude for as long as you can and allow your body to simply drink the silence. Of course, being in external silence but not internal silence doesn't fully allow for resetting the energy waves of your karma. If your mind wanders, let it wander to thoughts of gratitude and blessings toward your loved ones and the world. Transform every negative thought into a blessing towards others so that their lives are filled with grace.

Transforming karma necessitates being in a state of love and stillness. Love is a state of receptivity, humility, and seeing everything as an extension of oneself. There are times in life when our ego rears its head and we desire to prove our power through anger, hatred, or violence. There are times when we even feel we are more powerful than nature and wish to destroy it. But to effect a transformation of our karma, the greatest power is love. And for love to flow through us, we need to be receptive and allow grace to move through our body and life. The act of bowing down to all of creation is one of the greatest acts of humility that opens us up to grace and love. It is a great habit to develop through practice every morning when we wake up and every evening before going to bed: simply touch our head to the ground. We can also bow down while sitting on our bed.

We are connected with all of nature. When we have reverence for it, it naturally brings us into a state of harmony within. All of nature is alive and can support us in our path of life. We can connect with the earth to help us be more grounded rather than reactive in life. We can also connect with the earth to help ourselves let go some of the heavy emotions that we carry. Mountains can support us to feel more strength in our mind; the stars can support us for inspiration for our life visions; the sun can fill us with light to see clearly; and the sky can expand our perception to see our connection with all of life. When you meditate, you can imagine yourself like a mountain, like the sun, like the sky, like the earth. Merge with the aspect of nature that you feel you need the most or that you feel the most connected to.

Whereas meditation is being receptive and silent, prayer is sending energy out. The quality of our prayers is the quality of karma seeds that we plant. After sitting in meditation, it is a good practice to follow it with a few minutes of prayer, sending love, blessings, and gratitude for others and all of nature. Prayer should not be only for those whom you love and are close to you, but also for those who have hurt you and whom you might even feel hatred towards. The act of prayer transforms any residue of inner negativity into love. Pray for nature and for the entire earth to be filled with love. Pray in gratitude for the air that you breathe, the earth that you walk on, the food that nourishes you, and the water that purifies you and quenches your thirst. Gratitude is the greatest prayer. And gratitude is a tremendous power to transform karma for grace to come into your life.

It is not only through prayers and gratitude but also through ritualistic offerings that we make a gesture of giving back. In many of the ancient traditions, rituals were done on a daily basis with flowers, foods, incense, or seeds, to give an offering to the earth for one's life, for others' lives, for certain visions to become reality, and so much more. Giving is crucial in order to plant seeds to transform our life. It is an act of love and appreciation. It can be as simple as putting seeds or water out for the birds and animals on a daily basis. It can be a compliment that you give to someone to brighten their day. It can be giving food to a homeless person. Every day, make it a habit to give something, however big or small, from your heart to another.

Transforming your karma requires consistent awareness and actions that plant positive seeds. After some time of implementing some of the exercises advised throughout this book, take the time to review your written lists and consider how things have changed in your life. Look at the visions, or steps to your visions, that you have already accomplished. Reflect again on whether there are additional steps now that need to be done. Do you want to add any more ideas to your visions?

Reflect also on your inner self. Do you feel any different? Do you find there is any negative self-talk that is standing in your way? What are your own thoughts about yourself? All negative thoughts, even those concerning only yourself, are planting seeds of karma which keep you stuck. Loving yourself means being kind to yourself, just as you should be kind to others. When you are kind to yourself, it is easier to be kind to others because your self-love will overflow. Loving yourself also keeps your mind more peaceful by calming the waves of karma that can come with erratic negative thoughts. Another very important aspect of loving yourself is taking care of yourself. People often think that taking care of themselves has nothing to do with karma, yet it does, in a very profound way. When you take care of your body and maintain your health, those around you feel at peace knowing that you are doing well. However, not caring for yourself not only causes distress in your own life; it also creates a burden for those around you who will need to take care of you when your life or health goes through distress.

Your home, your body, your thoughts, your emotions, your words, and your actions all set the stage for the direction of your karma. Your offerings, forgiveness, prayers, peace of mind, humility, and gratitude are the keys to turning the wheel of your karma to a state of beauty and happiness.

Afterword

"Simplicity, patience, compassion.
These three are your greatest treasures.
Simple in actions and thoughts,
you return to the source of being.
Patient with both friends and enemies,
you accord with the way things are.
Compassionate toward yourself,
you reconcile all beings in the world."
— Lao Tzu, Tao Te Ching

K arma at its core is the realization that we are not isolated islands but interconnected. We are connected with all other human beings, animals, nature, and the entire universe. Every action, thought, and emotion that we have has repercussions. Life is energy expressed in different forms. Therefore, our lifestyle choices, our thoughts, our emotions, our words, and our actions

167

set the wheels of energy in motion on a specific path.

Karma is also defined as energy patterns that we create based on what we send out into the world. These patterns are partially inherited from our ancestors, but they are primarily the fruits of the seeds we ourselves have planted. When we are not happy with the direction that our life is going, it can feel like a curse has been placed on us. But if we think of it as such, it gives the power to an unknown force, as if we are mere helpless victims to our destiny. A powerful question to ask yourself when you are tempted to think of yourself as victim to misfortune is, *Have I inflicted the same misfortune on another?*

> ➤ If someone steals money from you: Did you ever take from someone something that was not yours?

> ➤ If someone shows unkindness toward you: Have you been unkind to others?

> ➤ If you are not valued: Have you not valued people in your life?

> ➤ If you are cheated on: Have you ever cheated on someone else?

These are just a few examples. But take the time to reflect on your own self or your family lineage to identify the root of the karma patterns.

Our karma depends greatly on how we perceive life. If we see ourselves as separate from our surroundings and other people, then we don't recognize how our actions are creating the reactions that we experience. In truth, everything and everyone is ultimately connected on a subtler level, therefore everything that we do reflects back to us, thereby creating our karma. Waves of our actions hit their target and reflect back either directly to us or through a detour, the source of which we may not recognize. Our perceptions set the ground for our thoughts and emotions, which in turn influence our reactions in life.

It is our past actions, thoughts, and emotions that have planted the seeds for the outcomes we are experiencing. The impact of thoughts and emotions are often overlooked, however, because they are not as tangible as words or actions. Once we begin to dig up the seeds of our past creation, we can prepare a fertile garden with new seeds that will grow and bear delicious fruits. Reflections on the past and offerings to amend our past are what transform our garden. When those seeds are of ancestral origin, just one person creating the change can impact the entire family moving forward; therefore, through the practice of greater awareness, catch yourself when your actions come from a place of ego and selfishness and could harm another. Instead, act with compassion, tolerance, patience, and love, sending out waves of peace throughout your life.

We all make mistakes out of ignorance. Thus we need to forgive others as well as ourselves, as harmful gestures towards others or ourselves will have repercussions. Neither should you love yourself at the expense of others, nor others at the expense of yourself. Love yourself and love others and accept your shortcomings as well as theirs. Love, compassion, prayer, and forgiveness return waves of similar quality, showering grace into our life.

Understanding that nature is an integral part of our life and existence, it is crucial to treat it with respect rather than as a resource to conquer. Nature is the greatest teacher of humility, harmony, and patience. In the same way that a tree does not discriminate who may pick its fruits, we need to see beauty everywhere. We need to clear the lens of our mind's eye to see that even the person who has deeply hurt us is simply ignorant of any other way of being. We all have made mistakes in our life.

In Hindu and Buddhist traditions, there is a terminology called *Ahimsa*, which means not doing harm to any being in thought, word, or deed. It means walking through life with gentleness and care and treating even a mosquito with the respect due a living being. When we put ourselves above everything and everyone, there is a tendency for the ego to run wild and, in doing so, to think that nothing we do will have repercussions. But we can't escape the laws of cause and effect. Under the law of the universe, everything has a right to exist.

To truly change our karma is to walk responsibly through the world. To recognize that every step we take, every thought we have, and our emotions, have consequences. If we keep our sight on the consequences, we see far and make our present decisions based on those rather than short-term benefits. To think that we are exempt from the law of karma is to live in an illusion that will come back to bite us in one form or another.

May you see love all around you, may your thoughts bring you peace, may your emotions be that of gratitude, and may your actions give the same to yourself and the world. May this book open a pathway for you to fill your life with grace, reaping your karma in the beautiful garden of your dreams.

With love,

Rita Panahi, L.Ac.

*"Wear gratitude like a cloak
and it will feed every corner of your life."*
— Rumi

Recommended Reading

Cheng Xinnong, Liangyue Deng, and Cheng Xinnong. Chinese Acupuncture and Moxibustion. China Books & Periodicals, Inc., 2000.

Judith, Anodea. Wheels of Life: A User's Guide to the Chakra System. Llewellyn Publications, 1987.

About the Author

R ita Panahi, L.Ac., Dipl.O.M., holds a master's in Chinese medicine. Over the past twenty-five years, she has had extensive training under renowned masters of the ancient teachings of the medicine, spiritual teachers, and numerous indigenous healers from various parts of the world.

She is the author of *Own Your Health Change Your Destiny*, *Lose Weight Unleash Your Creativity*, and her most recent book, *How to Change Your Karma Now*. Her knowledge has been compiled from her vast experience and travels over the years. She is licensed by the California Acupuncture Board, the New York Board, and the National Commission of Acupuncture and Oriental Medicine.

Also available by Rita Panahi, L.Ac.

Own Your Health Change Your Destiny

Also available by Rita Panahi, L.Ac.

Lose Weight Unleash Your Creativity

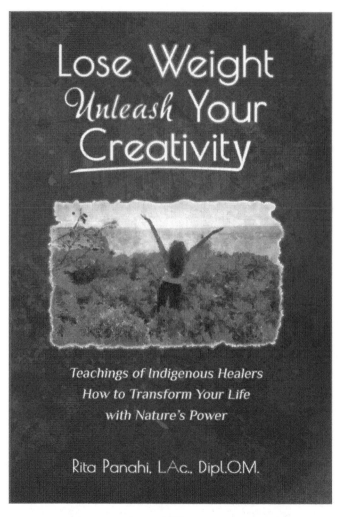

Stay Connected

http://www.facebook.com/RitaPanahiAuthor

https://www.facebook.com/groups/RitaPanahiAuthor

rita_lac

@RitaAuthor

www.ritapanahi.com

Made in the USA
San Bernardino,
CA